Seven Myths About Education

In this controversial new book, Daisy Christodoulou offers a thought-provoking critique of educational orthodoxy. Drawing on her recent experience of teaching in challenging schools, through a wide range of examples and case studies she shows just how much classroom practice contradicts basic scientific principles. She examines seven widely held beliefs which are holding back pupils and teachers:

- facts prevent understanding
- teacher-led instruction is passive
- the twenty-first century fundamentally changes everything
- you can always just look it up
- we should teach transferable skills
- projects and activities are the best way to learn
- teaching knowledge is indoctrination.

In each accessible and engaging chapter, Christodoulou sets out the theory of each myth, considers its practical implications and shows the worrying prevalence of such practice. Then, she explains exactly why it is a myth, with reference to the principles of modern cognitive science. She builds a powerful case explaining how governments and educational organisations around the world have let down teachers and pupils by promoting and even mandating evidence-less theory and bad practice.

This blisteringly incisive and urgent text is essential reading for all teachers, teacher training students, policy makers, headteachers, researchers and academics around the world.

Daisy Christodoulou is Research and Development Manager at ARK Schools, UK.

'This splendid, disinfecting book needs to be distributed gratis to every teacher, administrator, and college professor in the US' – **Professor E.D. Hirsch, eminent US scholar and former University of Virginia Professor of Education and Humanities**

'It is clear, from reading this book, that much of what is currently considered as "best practice" in schools, is in fact close to useless: at best merely a waste of time, and at worst an impediment to learning. [This book] is extremely controversial in the best way possible: it is correct' – **Tom Bennett, TES columnist, author and teacher, UK**

Seven Myths
About Education

Daisy Christodoulou

Routledge
Taylor & Francis Group

LONDON AND NEW YORK

The
Curriculum
Centre
CURRICULUM KNOW·HOW

First published 2014
by Routledge
2 Park Square, Milton Park, Abingdon, Oxon OX14 4RN

and by Routledge
711 Third Avenue, New York, NY 10017

Routledge is an imprint of the Taylor & Francis Group, an informa business

© 2014 D. Christodoulou

The right of D. Christodoulou to be identified as author of this
work has been asserted by her in accordance with sections 77
and 78 of the Copyright, Designs and Patents Act 1988.

Disclaimer: Every effort has been made to identify the owners of
copyrights and to obtain permission to reproduce copyrighted
material.

British Library Cataloguing in Publication Data
A catalogue record for this book is available from the British Library

Library of Congress Cataloging in Publication Data
Christodoulou, Daisy.
The seven myths about education / authored by Daisy
Christodoulou. -- First edition.
pages cm
ISBN 978-0-415-74681-6 (hardback) -- ISBN 978-0-415-74682-3
(pbk.) -- ISBN 978-1-315-79739-7 (e-book) 1. Education--
Research--Case studies. 2. Education--Philosophy--Case studies. I.
Title.
LB1028.C538 2014
370.7--dc23
2013038157

ISBN: 978-0-415-74681-6 (hbk)
ISBN: 978-0-415-74682-3 (pbk)
ISBN: 978-1-315-79739-7 (ebk)

Typeset in Bembo
by Saxon Graphics Ltd, Derby

Printed and bound in the United States of America by Publishers Graphics,
LLC on sustainably sourced paper.

The Curriculum Centre is a charitable organisation, founded to share the benefits of deep curriculum change. Its purpose is to help teachers and schools give pupils the foundational knowledge and skills they need to succeed in the 21st Century through effective and engaging content.

The Curriculum Centre has worked with national organisations, such as the Prince's Teaching Institute and the Specialist Schools and Academies Trust, and is currently leading a research pilot to improve reading comprehension skills through the teaching of History and Geography in primary aged pupils. The Word and World project is supported by the Education Endowment Foundation and is being evaluated by Durham University.

We welcome interest from teachers, leaders and schools ready to take a fresh look at their curriculum.

For more information visit: www.thecurriculumcentre.org

First Published June 2013

Published by The Curriculum Centre.
The Curriculum Centre, 11 Belgrave Road, London, SW1V 1RB
info@thecurriculumcentre.org
http://www.thecurriculumcentre.org

ISBN 978-0-9575919-0-5

The Curriculum Centre is part of Future Academies, registered
charity number 1123828. Future Academies is sponsored by
Future, registered charity number 1114396.

The views expressed are those of the author, not of The
Curriculum Centre

Contents

Foreword by Professor E.D. Hirsch

When this book first came out like a cleansing breeze from across the Atlantic Ocean to the USA, I wrote on the *Huffington Post* that it deserved "to be nominated as the "best book of 2013 on *American* education." I observed that there's little difference in the dominant educational ideas of the two countries, and that these ideas are accurately described as myths. The myths that Daisy Christodoulou identifies are anti-intellectual and (unwittingly) anti-egalitarian. By disparaging facts and knowledge they simultaneously lower overall school achievement and widen the gap between haves and have-nots.

Social science research in the United States has shown a consistent correlation between income and vocabulary size. Students who have been read to as toddlers, and who understand the language of the classroom are constantly building up their knowledge and vocabulary in school. Those who come from less advantaged homes enter school without the verbal repertoire and knowledge that enable them to thrive. Instead, they fall further behind more fortunate children.

This widening of the gap can be reversed by systematic knowledge building in the school – as 25 years of evidence from Core Knowledge schools has shown. But no such good result can come from incoherent curricula and teachers who have been indoctrinated in anti-fact myths.

When this book came out in digital form last year, the educational establishment on both sides of the Atlantic criticized it vigorously for creating "straw men." What good teachers believed was much more subtle, so they said, which was that facts in isolation worked against "understanding," and that teacher-led teaching led to passivity. The slogans which have caused the anti-fact ideas to persist have been refined and field tested for a hundred years. Subtle rhetorical adjustments have been made in their manner of presentation, enabling the defenders of the status quo to claim that Ms Christodoulou is describing "straw men!" No sensible person, they respond, ever actually said that "facts prevent understanding." Now it's true that no one ever puts it in just that blunt way. Rather, the idea is implied by persistently repeating the principle that facts are much less important than "understanding." This book's strength is in the way it exposes this linguistic legerdemain by analysing in detail the classroom practice it inspires. For all their rhetorical refinements, in practice too many in the educational establishment really do minimise and deride the teaching of facts.

As Ms Christodoulou says, far from attacking a straw man, she is attacking what is openly described as 'best practice'. She has amply documented her analysis, setting forth each myth not in her own words but by direct quotations from recognized authorities. She then describes how each idea actually has worked in practice, and she presents an account of the relevant research in cognitive psychology that overwhelmingly debunks the guiding idea or myth. It's all presented with clarity, earnestness, and wit, from a person who has been a classroom teacher, and who has seen in action the tragic failures of these dominant ideas.

Those myths have one enormous drawback. They are empirically incorrect. They don't conform to how the mind works. They exhibit just enough apparent truth and attractiveness to have won the minds and hearts of teachers for nearly a hundred years. That's why this book is so very important. As a forceful, well-researched book by a teacher, it may persuade other teachers as well as the general public. In the contemporary world we can no longer afford the ineffectual and inegalitarian education induced by these well-meant but disastrous conceptual mistakes.

Foreword by Dylan Wiliam

For the last decade or so, politicians and policymakers of all complexions have advocated a view that education should be more strongly based on research evidence about "what works" in promoting student learning. The idea is that if only we could make education more like medicine, then everything would be fine. There are two problems with this. Firstly, it is now clear that medicine is much less "research-based" than most people imagine, with practice based as much on the basis of historical practice, or flawed research studies, as it is on what really helps improve health and wellbeing (Goldacre, 2012). Second, when education is contrasted negatively with medicine, the examples being used are usually highly selective. We have had huge successes in combatting diseases such as polio and smallpox, but we know far less about issues such as how to get people to adhere to drug regimes that will help them survive.

What is particularly ironic in all this is that there is now a substantial amount of knowledge about what happens when learning takes place, and what kinds of school experiences are likely to help students make the greatest progress, and yet very little of this research evidence makes its way into classrooms. Many university departments of education do not have a single psychologist, and most teacher preparation programmes include little or no psychology of education. As a result, it is entirely possible for someone to qualify as a teacher and have no knowledge about recent, and even not so recent, advances in cognitive psychology.

For example, there is now a considerable body of evidence that discovery learning approaches—where students "discover things for themselves"—is simply less effective than those where the students are guided by a teacher to the intended learning outcomes (Mayer 2004). This does not mean that students should be passive recipients of knowledge—the idea that learning is an active rather than a passive process has been well established for over half-a-century—but activity is not the same as engagement. In too many classrooms, teachers worry about having the students active rather than having the students thinking, and even where students are thinking, there is often too little concern for what students are thinking *about*.

We also know that just getting teachers to talk less, and have students talk more is unlikely to improve learning in classrooms. For example, in the TIMSS video studies of middle-school mathematics classrooms, it was discovered that in US classrooms (which for these purposes are very similar to UK classrooms), there were approximately 8 teacher words for every student word. In Japanese middle schools, the figure was 13, and for Hong Kong, it was 16.

This disconnect between what cognitive science has revealed about learning and what happens in our classrooms has for me been a growing source of unease for many years, and then a few months ago, I came across Daisy Christodoulou's wonderful book. I had been asked for my opinion on the book by someone who regarded it as heretical, and so, one Sunday morning, I downloaded it on to my Kindle and began reading it.

I wasn't sure what to expect. Too many books that claim to expose "myths" about something or other start out by erecting straw men—claims that no-one really believed in the first place, or are so specific that they can easily be disproved—and then demolishing them. What it refreshing about *Seven Myths About Education* is that the myths presented really are widely held, and what's more the book goes into considerable detail to show evidence that they are endorsed at the highest levels of our education system. And then, with brilliant analysis, Daisy Christodoulou provides rigorous scientific evidence that each of these myths is just that—something that is just demonstrably wrong. It is also beautifully written.

In my view, this may well be the most important book of the decade on teaching (and I reluctantly include my own works in this assessment). It should be required reading on every teacher training course, and schools that are genuinely interested in unleashing the power of education to transform the lives of young people should buy a copy for every teacher. I've never said that about a book before, but that's how good I think *Seven Myths About Education* is.

References

Hiebert, J., Gallimore, R., Garnier, H., Givvin, K.B., Hollingsworth, H., Jacobs, J.K., Stigler, J.W. (2003). *Teaching mathematics in seven countries: Results from the TIMSS 1999 Video Study* (Vol. NCES (2003–013)). Washington, DC: National Center for Education Statistics.

Mayer, R.E. (2004). Should there be a three-strikes rule against pure discovery learning? The case for guided methods on instruction. *American Psychologist, 59*(1), 14-19.

Acknowledgements

Many people have helped me write this book. Caroline Nash offered valuable advice, support and encouragement and also gave me a sabbatical from my work at the Curriculum Centre. Jo Saxton, Anastasia de Waal, Maria Egan, Michelle Major and Joe Kirby all read drafts of the book and offered valuable suggestions and ideas. Syd Egan provided the cricket and baseball comparison in Chapter 4. Sonia Cutler edited and proofread the manuscript.

Any mistakes that remain are, of course, my own responsibility.

Introduction

My mother and father are both intelligent people who grew up in the East End of London. They both left school young, with few formal qualifications. Although they have had happy and fulfilled lives, I think they have both wondered at various points in their life what might have been if they had been pushed and encouraged at school. I see people of my parents' age in the news all the time who are no more innately intelligent than them, but who, thanks to different circumstances of birth and education, have had many more opportunities in life. Education matters. And in modern Britain, all the statistics tell us that we are not much closer to a fair distribution of educational opportunity than we were in my parents' day. For example, a 2010 report by the Equalities and Human Rights Commission states that 'educational attainment continues to be strongly associated with socio-economic background', that 'students eligible for FSM [free school meals] are only half as likely to have good GCSE results as those who are not' and that 'the proportion of young people entering higher education from lower socio-economic groups … remains substantially below that of those from professional backgrounds'.[1]

Research by the Sutton Trust confirms these findings, showing that while educational inequalities are established before a pupil starts school, 'the inequalities continue to widen in school: two thirds of pupils on free school meals who are among the top fifth of performers at age 11 are not among the top fifth of performers at GCSE, and half do not go on to university'.[2] Although the numbers attending higher education (HE) institutions have increased dramatically since the 1960s, there is evidence that this expansion has disproportionately benefited the already wealthy. In 2003, Blanden and Machin argued that HE expansion 'has actually acted to significantly widen participation gaps between rich and poor children'.[3]

Like my parents, I grew up in East London and went to my local primary school. At 11, I got an assisted place which paid the fees for me to go to a private school. At 18, I went to the University of Warwick to study English Literature. From the moment I got the assisted place, I was well aware of how fortunate and privileged I was. When I graduated from university, one of the reasons why I decided to train as a teacher was to try to share the good luck and privilege I had had with others. I trained through Teach First in 2007 and was placed in a secondary school in London soon after. I taught there for three years and enjoyed it immensely. However, day after day I would be confronted with astonishing evidence of the pupils' low levels of basic skills and knowledge.

When I talked to colleagues at other schools, they had similar experiences. We were all teaching in particularly challenging schools, admittedly, so our experience is not completely representative. However, from the research I have done since, I do not think that what we encountered was that exceptional. On the subject of basic skills, research from the University of Sheffield shows that 22 per cent of 16–19-year-olds have serious problems with numeracy and 17 per cent have similar problems with literacy.[4] Mathematically, the adults in this category have 'very basic competence in maths, mainly limited to arithmetical computations and some ability to comprehend and use other forms of mathematical information'.[5] The report gives some examples of the types of maths questions that can be too tricky for people in this category:

> Subtract 1.78 from 5.
> Take away 2.43 from 5.
> Number of apples each person gets if a box of 72 is shared by six people.
> Work out 15% of 700.
> Number of children in a crowd of 7900 if the proportion is 10%.
> What is 5/6 of 300?[6]

The weak literacy that defines this category is 'people at this level can handle only simple tests and straightforward questions on them where no distracting information is adjacent or nearby'.[7] The report does not give any concrete examples of exactly the kinds of tasks people in this category are unable to accomplish. I would put forward my own example. I have given the 2009 Welsh Joint Education Committee Foundation GCSE English Paper 2 to several classes of pupils.[8] It features a series of comprehension questions on a leaflet from the Royal National Lifeboat Institution (RNLI) (see Figure 1.1).

One of the questions that followed was: 'List two things you will receive if you become a member of the RNLI.' Several pupils who sat this paper responded 'A lifeboat'. This was an actual GCSE paper and the examiners' report confirms that my pupils were not alone in making this inference: 'A number of markers were also told that if they became members of the RNLI, they would receive a lifeboat in return!'[9] I think this is what the Sheffield researchers mean when they speak of pupils who can only answer 'straightforward questions … where no distracting information is adjacent or nearby'.[10]

As far as I know, there has been no similarly robust investigation into the type of knowledge school-leavers have and do not have. There is certainly no evidence that contradicts my anecdotal impressions, and there is some,

When you come on board as a member ...

... you will benefit too.

The Lifeboat – your quarterly magazine

As an RNLI member, every three months you will receive the latest issue of this exclusive magazine, keeping you in touch with the rescuers – and the rescued.

Individual Shoreline membership costs £18; Joint Shoreline membership – for partners – costs £30.

You can also 'fly the flag' for our volunteer lifeboat crews wherever you go, with this attractive window sticker – exclusively for members.

Figure 1.1 Text from a Royal National Lifeboat Institution's leaflet used in the 2009 Welsh Joint Education Committee Foundation English Paper 2.

admittedly less robust, evidence that confirms it. An informal survey done by the history professor Derek Matthews is particularly revealing as he questioned pupils at the other end of the educational scale from the ones I taught.[11] He asked his first-year history undergraduates five fairly basic questions about British history; 89 per cent of them could not name a nineteenth-century British prime minister while 70 per cent did not know where the Boer Wars were fought. If that is what Russell Group undergraduates *do not* know, then what can we assume that the 40 per cent of school-leavers who fail to get five A★–Cs at GCSE *do* know? In my experience and that of many of my colleagues, very little.

I want to give a few examples of what pupils don't know in order to illustrate this problem. My aim in giving these examples is not to mock or insult these pupils. Far from it: a central aim of this book is to show that the reason why these pupils have such poor skills and know so little is because we have failed to teach them those important skills and knowledge. If these examples are meant to shame anyone, it is to shame all of us involved in education. But rather than apportioning blame, the real reason why I have included these examples is to give some kind of an idea about the concrete reality behind the figures and statistics that are often quoted. Before I became a teacher, I would read reports about a certain percentage of school-leavers being unable to read, and I would tut and then turn to the next page in the paper. By giving these examples, I want to try to explain what the actual reality of these statistics is. I have taught many pupils who could not place London, their home city, on a map of Britain or their local area on a map of London. Many could not name the date of any significant historical event. Their understanding of the difference between continents and countries was weak – plenty thought Africa was a country. Plenty did not understand the difference between England and Great Britain; plenty could not name the four countries that make up the UK. They seemed to know vaguely that in the distant past cars, aeroplanes, computers and telephones did not exist, but they had little idea about how people travelled and communicated before their invention. Most of my pupils had heard of America and Australia, but many of them were unaware that there was a time when English-speaking people did not live there. Many were also unaware of the origins of basic foods such as milk, bread and potatoes. It seems to me that pupils who do not know these things are at a disadvantage.

Let me make one thing clear: I am not claiming that there was some golden age of English education. Things may not be perfect now, but I would not for a second argue that they were in the past. The main aim of this book is to show how we need to change education based on the discoveries of modern science. The exemplars I refer to are not from England 50 years ago but from high-performing countries today. When I began teaching, I knew full well that the education system which failed my parents was deeply flawed. I had naively assumed that in the interim, it would have improved greatly. The Sheffield research showed that the proportions of pupils failing to achieve those basic literacy and numeracy skills had not changed much over the decades. Research by Michael Shayer suggests that pupils' problem-solving skills have stagnated or even regressed over the last few decades, too.[12]

I have never worked so hard in my life as in my first year of teaching, and I doubt I ever will again. All my colleagues worked ceaselessly, too. Some politicians liked to blame us for being lazy and having low expectations, but I knew that we were not lacking effort or good intentions. And yet so many of our pupils left us unable to read or write properly, and with the kind of ignorance I have described previously. What on earth were we doing wrong?

What I want to suggest here is that the problem is one of content, not structures. This is an unpopular view. Politically, both those on the right and on the left prefer structural solutions to education problems. The right ask for teachers to work harder and for a return to academic selection; the left ask for genuine comprehensives and for more money for schools. Over the last decade, the biggest reforms in English schools have involved the way schools are governed and managed. The first few New Labour academies allowed for schools to exist outside of the control of local authorities; the current coalition government have allowed many more schools to become academies and have also allowed new free schools to be set up by groups of parents and educators. These reforms are undoubtedly important and deserving of debate and scrutiny. But they are about one very small aspect of education reform, and in all the heat and controversy about school structures, much else that matters gets lost. In particular, we pay too little attention to the actual content of lessons: what gets taught and how it is taught. In the end, that is what education is about. Anyone who wishes to change school structures should see this not as a good in itself, but as a means to the end of improving the actual content of education, of making what actually happens in the classroom better than it was before. However, I fear that in all the debates about school structures, we have come to consider these changes as an end in themselves. In this book, I want to shift the focus back on to what actually happens in the classroom.

My central argument is that much of what teachers are taught about education is wrong, and that they are encouraged to teach in ineffective ways. After I had been teaching for three years, I took a year out to do further study. I was shocked to stumble across an entire field of educational and scientific research which completely disproved so many of the theories I had been taught when training and teaching. I was not just shocked; I was angry. I felt as though I had been misled. I had been working furiously for three years, teaching hundreds of lessons, and much information that would have made my life a whole lot easier and would have helped my pupils immeasurably had just never been introduced to me. Worse, ideas that had absolutely no evidence backing them up had been presented to me as unquestionable axioms. One of the writers I most enjoyed reading was Herbert Simon. His research into decision-making won him a Nobel Prize. Together with two other cognitive scientists, he wrote a paper criticising many of the ideas that are popular in US education:

> New 'theories' of education are introduced into schools every day (without labeling them as experiments) on the basis of their philosophical or common-sense plausibility but without genuine empirical support.[13]

Many of the experiments and evidenceless theories he saw in US schools are unfortunately also present in the English education system.

In this book, I outline what I think the seven most damaging of these myths are. There is a chapter on each one. In each chapter, I have gone to great lengths to prove that this particular myth is indeed prevalent in education, and more specifically, in schools. This is because in discussions I have had about these topics, lots of people have simply refused to believe my descriptions of what things are like in schools. The most frequent objection I have faced is that I have isolated some examples of bad practice and generalised from them; or, in other terms, I am attacking a straw man. Nothing could be further from the truth. The kind of practice I am attacking in this book is what many education authorities consider to be the very best practice. For every myth I have identified, I have found concrete and robust examples of how this myth has influenced classroom practice across England. Only then do I go on to show why it is a myth and why it is so damaging.

When proving that these myths exist and are influential, I have considered two main categories of evidence. The first is theoretical: I have tried to find the philosophical roots of these myths. In some chapters, this involves going back decades or even centuries; in other chapters, I have looked at what current theorists are saying. The second category is practical. This mainly involves looking at recent publications of government advice to teachers, popular teacher training manuals and articles in the educational press. Here, I have leant very heavily on subject reports from the Office for Standards in Education, Children's Services and Skills (Ofsted). I explain the full rationale for using such reports in Chapter 2, but briefly, these reports are based on national inspection data and provide detailed descriptions of classroom practice. It would have been easy to have found similar descriptions of similar classroom practice from a variety of other sources, and indeed, I do use some examples from such sources, but none of these have the authority and range of Ofsted's judgements. Only once I have established the prevalence of a practice do I give anecdotal explanations of my own experience with it.

I know that there are many people who think that only practical evidence matters. I disagree. To understand the actions of practical people, I think we need to examine their underlying philosophical rationale. On this point, I have been much influenced by John Maynard Keynes's famous explanation of the power of ideas:

> The ideas of economists and political philosophers, both when they are right and when they are wrong, are more powerful than is commonly understood. Indeed the world is ruled by little else. Practical men, who believe themselves to be quite exempt from any intellectual influence, are usually the slaves of some defunct economist.[14]

I am interested in tracing ideas, not the citations of names. It is entirely possible to be influenced by the ideas of someone you have never heard of. Most of the Ofsted inspectors I have met present themselves as very practical and hard-headed people. Many of them may never have read or even heard of theorists such as Paulo Freire. But I would still contend that they are deeply influenced by such defunct theorists. In this book, I try to trace the links between theories and modern practice. Explaining what a theory means in practice is important, because I think that when you read theories on their own, they often have a surface plausibility that is convincing. Before I became a teacher, I read many vague theories about Google changing the way we think that I found very persuasive. But I was never forced to fully consider the practical implications of these theories. The other reason why it is important to consider the practical implications of a theory is that it makes having a debate about the issue clearer. Theories can often be couched in vague and unclear terms. Sometimes it is not always clear exactly what they mean. Richard Hofstadter noticed that this was the case with John Dewey:

> It is commonly said that Dewey was misunderstood, and it is repeatedly pointed out that in time he had to protest against some of the educational practices carried on in his name. Perhaps his intent was widely, even regularly violated, but Dewey was hard to read and interpret. He wrote prose of terrible vagueness and plasticity ... that this style is, perhaps symptomatically, at its worst in Dewey's most important educational writings suggests that his great influence as an educational spokesman may have been derived in some part from the very inaccessibility of his exact meanings ... Serious faults in style are rarely, if ever, matters of 'mere' style; they embody real difficulties in conception. Far more probable than the thesis that Dewey was perversely distorted by obtuse or overenthusiastic followers is the idea that the unresolved problems of interpretation to which his work gave rise were tokens of real ambiguities and gaps in thought.[15]

I have found this to be true not just of Dewey but of many modern educationalists. Often, I would read articles by theorists who would spend an entire essay denigrating the ideas of facts and fact-learning, and then include a throwaway line at the end like 'of course I do not mean that you should not teach facts'. Then I would look at the practice they recommended and see that, actually, it really did involve not teaching facts. So, by looking at what these theories and theorists recommend in practice, we have a firmer basis for debate and discussion.

The seven myths I have identified are as follows:

1   facts prevent understanding
2   teacher-led instruction is passive
3   the twenty-first century fundamentally changes everything
4   you can always just look it up
5   we should teach transferable skills
6   projects and activities are the best way to learn
7   teaching knowledge is indoctrination.

Collectively, some would say that these myths are examples of progressive education. I reject this label. First, there is nothing at all progressive about myths. Second, as I show in Chapter 7, there has never been unanimity of agreement from progressives about these ideas. Third, the word progressive implies newness and originality. There is nothing new about any of these ideas. They have been around for decades, sometimes longer. The progress we are making in discovering how humans learn actually discredits these ideas.

If I had to come up with a word or phrase to sum up the intellectual rationale behind these myths, then I would prefer educational formalism, as many of these myths work on the assumption that form is more important than substance. If I had to come up with an intellectual trend that underpins them, then I would choose postmodernism, not progressivism. Postmodernism is sceptical about the value of truth and knowledge, and many of these myths have at their heart a deep scepticism about the value of knowledge. It is for this reason that I begin with myth 1 (facts prevent understanding) and 2 (teacher-led instruction is passive). These could be said to be the foundation myths of all the others discussed in this book. They have a long pedigree and they provide the theoretical justification for so much of what goes on in schools. The next two myths, that the twenty-first century fundamentally changes everything and that you can always just look it up, are essentially modern justifications for myth 1. Myth 5, that we should teach transferable skills, is another justification for not teaching knowledge. Myth 6 is about pedagogy; it suggests ways of organising the classroom that reduce the transmission of knowledge. The final myth is about the political aspect of knowledge: it suggests that teaching knowledge is akin to brainwashing. Taken together, all seven myths damage the education of our pupils.

Notes

1   Equalities and Human Rights Commission. How fair is Britain? Equality, human rights and good relations in 2010. The first triennial review (2011), pp. 300, 325, 340, www.equalityhumanrights.com/uploaded_files/triennial_review/how_fair_is_britain_-_complete_report.pdf (accessed 3 March 2013).

2   The Sutton Trust. *Increasing Higher Education Participation Amongst Disadvantaged Young People and Schools in Poor Communities: Report to the National Council for Educational Excellence.* London: Sutton Trust, 2008, p. 5.

3   Blanden, J. and Machin, S. Educational inequality and the expansion of UK higher education. *Scottish Journal of Political Economy* 2004; 51: 230–249.

4   Brooks, G. and Rashid, S. The levels of attainment in literacy and numeracy of 13- to 19-year-olds in England, 1948–2009 (2010), p. 6, www.nrdc.org.uk/publications_details.asp?ID=181# (accessed 3 March 2013).

5   Ibid., p. 8.

6   Ibid., p. 52.

7   Ibid., p. 64.

8   Welsh Joint Education Committee (CBAC). GCSE, 150/02, English Foundation Tier Paper 2, P.M. Thursday, 4 June 2009 (2009), www.sprowstonhigh.org/cms/resources/revision/English/2009%20Summer%20Foundation%20-%20RNLI.pdf (accessed 3 March 2013).

9   Welsh Joint Education Committee (CBAC). GCSE examiners' reports, English and English Literature, Summer 2009 (2009), p. 18, www.wjec.co.uk/uploads/publications/9063.pdf (accessed 3 March 2012).

10 Brooks, G. and Rashid, S. The levels of attainment in literacy and numeracy of 13- to 19-year-olds in England, 1948–2009 (2010), p. 64, www.nrdc.org.uk/publications_details.asp?ID=181# (accessed 3 March 2013).

11 Matthews, D. The strange death of history teaching (fully explained in seven easy-to-follow lessons) (2009), p. 33, www.heacademy.ac.uk/assets/documents/subjects/history/br_matthews_deathofhistory_20090803.pdf (accessed 3 March 2010).

12 Shayer, M., Ginsburg, D. and Coe, R. Thirty years on – a large anti-Flynn effect? The Piagetian test Volume & Heaviness norms 1975–2003. *British Journal of Educational Psychology* 2007; 77 (Pt 1): 25–41.

13 Anderson, J.R., Reder, L.M. and Simon, H.A. Applications and misapplications of cognitive psychology to mathematics education. *Texas Education Review* 2000; 1: 29–49.

14 Keynes, J.M. *The General Theory of Employment, Interest, and Money.* New York: Harcourt, Brace & World, 1964, p. 383.

15 Hofstadter, R. *Anti-Intellectualism in American Life.* New York: Vintage Books, 1973, p. 361.

Myth 1

Facts prevent understanding

Where is the evidence that people believe this and that it has affected education policy and classroom practice?

Theoretical evidence

Perhaps the earliest expression of the idea that learning facts will not bring true understanding came from the Swiss philosopher Jean-Jacques Rousseau in the eighteenth century. In *Émile, or Education*, he advises that you should 'give your scholar no verbal lessons; he should be taught by experience alone'.[1] The reason for this is that learning facts is ineffective: 'What is the use of inscribing on their brains a list of symbols which mean nothing to them?'[2] The pupil might be able to repeat exactly what you have told them, but they will not be able to use the facts they have been told or understand how those facts can be deployed in different ways:

> You tell me they acquire some rudiments of geometry, and you think you prove your case; not so, it is mine you prove; you show that far from being able to reason themselves, children are unable to retain the reasoning of others; for if you follow the method of these little geometricians you will see they only retain the exact impression of the figure and the terms of the demonstration. They cannot meet the slightest new objection; if the figure is reversed they can do nothing.[3]

Not only is such fact-learning ineffective; it is also immoral. In rendering the pupil passive, it not only ensures they are not learning, it ensures they are having all the joy and excitement of childhood knocked out of them:

> No, if nature has given the child this plasticity of brain which fits him to receive every kind of impression, it was not that you should imprint on it the names and dates of kings, the jargon of heraldry, the globe and geography, all those words without present meaning or future use for the child, which flood of words overwhelms his sad and barren childhood.[4]

In the late nineteenth century, the educationalist John Dewey also emphasised experience and the importance of learning by doing. Rousseau thought the child 'should be taught by experience alone'; the phrase most commonly associated with Dewey is learning by doing. For Dewey, the problem with many of the schools in his time was that the pupils were not active:

> The child is thrown into a passive, receptive or absorbing attitude. The conditions are such that he is not permitted to follow the law of his nature; the result is friction and waste.[5]

We see it again; teaching facts makes the pupil passive; making the pupil passive means they must ignore their natural inclinations; ignoring their natural inclinations makes them unhappy and does not help them to learn. And again, the problem is with teaching facts to the pupil:

> We present the child with arbitrary symbols. Symbols are a necessity in mental development, but they have their place as tools for economising effort; presented by themselves they are a mass of meaningless and arbitrary ideas imposed from without.[6]

Paulo Freire was a Brazilian educator whose most famous book, *Pedagogy of the Oppressed*, was written in 1970. Like Dewey, his theories have enjoyed great influence: *Pedagogy of the Oppressed* has sold over one million copies worldwide.[7] It was undoubtedly more popular in its 1970s heyday, but a measure of its continuing influence can be seen by the fact that it came tenth in a Teachers' TV survey in 2007 to find the most inspirational education books.[8] Freire also criticises how facts prevent pupils from truly understanding the reality around them:

> The teacher … expounds on a topic completely alien to the existential experience of the students. His task is to 'fill' the students with the contents of his narration—contents which are detached from reality, disconnected from the totality that engendered them and could give them significance.[9]

He developed his famous banking concept of education, illustrating how facts prevent understanding:

> Education thus becomes an act of depositing, in which the students are the depositories and the teacher is the depositor. Instead of communicating, the teacher issues communiqués and makes deposits which the students patiently receive, memorise, and repeat. This is the 'banking' concept of education, in which the scope of action allowed to the students extends only as far as receiving, filing, and storing the deposits. They do, it is true, have the opportunity to become collectors or cataloguers of the things

they store. But in the last analysis, it is the people themselves who are filed away through the lack of creativity, transformation, and knowledge in this (at best) misguided system.[10]

All these metaphors should remind us of another famous writer on education, Charles Dickens. Although Dickens was a novelist, not an educationalist, his works and characters are so famous and influential that they merit mention here. His depiction of Thomas Gradgrind's school at the start of *Hard Times* is a literary masterpiece:

> Now, what I want is, Facts. Teach these boys and girls nothing but Facts. Facts alone are wanted in life. Plant nothing else, and root out everything else. You can only form the minds of reasoning animals upon Facts: nothing else will ever be of any service to them. This is the principle on which I bring up my own children, and this is the principle on which I bring up these children. Stick to Facts, sir! …
>
> The speaker, and the schoolmaster, and the third grown person present, all backed a little, and swept with their eyes the inclined plane of little vessels then and there arranged in order, ready to have imperial gallons of facts poured into them until they were full to the brim.[11]

As we can see, the metaphor at the end has very much in common with those metaphors used by Rousseau, Freire and Dewey. Dickens criticises those people who would view children as passive receptacles to be filled with facts. The rest of the novel makes it clear what happens to children subjected to Gradgrind's methods. They turn into emotionally stunted and broken adults, like his daughter Louisa, or into emotionless, heartless snitches like Bitzer. *Hard Times*, incidentally, came seventh in the same inspirational books on education poll previously mentioned. It is also striking to note how often the name Gradgrind is mentioned in serious discussions on education. The current affairs programme *Newsnight* recently used a lengthy clip of a TV version to illustrate a feature on exam reform.[12] Comparing a teacher or anyone involved in education to Gradgrind is an insult, suggesting that the teacher is both emotionally stunted and doing great emotional damage to their pupils.

One common trope is seen in all of these writers. They all set up polar opposites between facts, which are generally seen as bad, and something else, which is generally seen as good. Facts are opposed with meaning, understanding, reasoning, significance and, in Dickens's case, fancy or what we might today call imagination or creativity. If you want pupils to understand the true meaning of something, to be able to reason, and to be creative and imaginative, then facts are not the way to achieve such an aim.

Sometimes, it is argued that these theorists were not hostile to facts *per se*, merely to certain prescriptive and artificial methods of learning such facts. In Chapter 2, I shall consider this argument in full and look in closer detail at the practices these theorists preferred instead of fact-learning. But for now, I just want to consider their attitudes towards facts themselves, and I think it is fair to say that both their arguments and the language they use show that they are deeply uneasy about the very idea of facts.

Modern practice

At first sight, it might seem as though these ideas are about as far away from the modern education system as possible. After all, are we not being frequently told how stressed our pupils are? How many exams they have to sit? How awful and joyless their childhoods are? Surely the problem here is exactly the one that Rousseau and the others diagnosed: too much fact-learning. It is indeed true that our pupils have to sit very many exams. It may well be true, as the United Nations claim, that they are the unhappiest in the developed world.[13] But their problems most certainly do not derive from being overloaded with facts; actually, as I want to show now, current educational practice is guided very clearly by the ideas I have outlined previously.

There are two main ways in which we can trace the influence of such ideas: in the curriculum that teachers are told to deliver and in the pedagogical techniques that they are trained and told to use. We can reliably know the curriculum teachers are statutorily required to deliver by looking at publications of the National Curriculum (NC) for England and associated documents. We can reliably trace the pedagogical techniques that are used in English schools by looking at the reports and other publications of the Office for Standards in Education, Children's Services and Skills (Ofsted), the English schools inspectorate. In this chapter, I shall look just at the NC; the following chapters will consider the publications by Ofsted.

First, I shall consider the reliability and significance of the NC as a source, which is fairly easy to prove. Since it was introduced in 1988, maintained schools in England have been statutorily required to deliver it. So if we find that the NC does, or does not, require something, then that is significant.

In the primary curriculum, last revised in 1999, and the Key Stage 3 (KS3) curriculum, last revised in 2007, there is a deliberate reduction, and in some cases complete removal, of subject content. This move was sometimes taken to mean that the curriculum freed up teachers to teach what they liked. This was not quite the case. While these curricula certainly had very much less prescribed subject content, they still had a great deal of prescription. But in this case, the prescription was for skills, experiences and certain methods, rather than content. Consider the history curriculum, for example. The 2007 KS3 curriculum prescribes not knowledge but instead a list of skills. The things that pupils should learn are as follows:

Historical enquiry
Pupils should be able to:

a   identify and investigate, individually and as part of a team, specific historical questions or issues, making and testing hypotheses
b   reflect critically on historical questions or issues.

Using evidence
Pupils should be able to:
a   identify, select and use a range of historical sources, including textual, visual and oral sources, artefacts and the historic environment
b   evaluate the sources used in order to reach reasoned conclusions.

Communicating about the past
Pupils should be able to:
a   present and organise accounts and explanations about the past that are coherent, structured and substantiated, using chronological conventions and historical vocabulary
b   communicate their knowledge and understanding of history in a variety of ways, using chronological conventions and historical vocabulary.[14]

Most subjects in the 2007 curriculum are like this. For example, here are the essential skills and processes of the science curriculum, which are actually remarkably similar to the history skills:

Practical and enquiry skills
Pupils should be able to:
a   use a range of scientific methods and techniques to develop and test ideas and explanations
b   assess risk and work safely in the laboratory, field and workplace
c   plan and carry out practical and investigative activities, both individually and in groups.

Critical understanding of evidence
Pupils should be able to:
a   obtain, record and analyse data from a wide range of primary and secondary sources, including ICT sources, and use their findings to provide evidence for scientific explanations
b   evaluate scientific evidence and working methods.

Communication
Pupils should be able to:
a   use appropriate methods, including ICT, to communicate scientific information and contribute to presentations and discussions about scientific issues.[15]

The key concepts for most subjects follow a similar format: enquiry, evidence, communication. The guidance that comes with this curriculum states clearly that there is deliberately 'less prescribed subject content' and, instead, more of a 'focus on the key concepts and processes that underlie each subject'.[16] Here we see the opposition that we saw Dewey, Rousseau and Freire make. They opposed facts and understanding; the curriculum opposes subject content and subject concepts. Just as with Dewey, Rousseau and Freire, the rhetoric used in the NC documents also reveals unease about facts and knowledge. In the explanation of the intended outcomes of the curriculum, the words 'knowledge' and 'facts' were not used once:

> The aim is to develop a coherent 11–19 curriculum that builds on young people's experiences in the primary phase and that helps all young people to become successful learners, confident individuals and responsible citizens. Specifically, the curriculum is intended to help young people to:
>
> - Achieve high standards and make better progress
> - Narrow the gap and enable those not achieving age-related expectations at age 11 to catch up with their peers
> - Have and be able to use high-quality personal, learning and thinking skills (PLTS) and become independent learners
> - Have and be able to use high-quality functional skills
> - Be challenged and stretched to achieve their potential
> - Have increased commitment to and enjoyment of learning leading to participation to 19 and beyond.[17]

And in the curriculum's foreword, Mick Waters, the man who was largely responsible for it, said this:

> The curriculum should be treasured. There should be real pride in our curriculum: the learning that the nation has decided to set before its young.[18]

There is something a bit odd about this statement. It is the way that learning is used as a noun. It sounds unnatural to set learning before someone, and it would sound more logical to set knowledge before them. I think this can be seen as another example of how uneasy Waters and the other drafters of this curriculum were about the very idea of knowledge.

Mick Waters was Director of Curriculum at the Qualifications and Curriculum Authority, the organisation responsible for this curriculum, from 2005 to 2009. Peter Wilby, the *Guardian* education columnist, argues that Waters 'has probably changed secondary schooling more profoundly than anybody in the past 20 years'.[19] He bases this judgement mainly on his role in creating the 2007 curriculum. If we look at Waters's influences when he was drafting the curriculum, they can tell us more about his attitude to knowledge and fact-learning. He contributed a positive foreword to a publication by the Association of Teachers and Lecturers (ATL) titled *Subject to Change*. That publication calls for a Deweyan curriculum in which pupils should receive lessons in walking, digging and planting wheat and 'where rote learning of facts must give way to nurturing through education of essential transferable skills'.[20] In March 2012, Waters gave an interview to the ATL in which he said that education 'doesn't have to be this endless transmission of information'.[21]

Unlike the KS3 curriculum, the primary curriculum has not been revised since 1999. But similarly, it makes the skills and processes of each subject statutory, while the facts and knowledge are optional and described in much broader and vaguer terms. It is fair to say, therefore, that the NC as it currently stands draws an opposition between facts and conceptual understanding and is sceptical of the value of facts.

The progression of skills included within the NC framework is quite similar to that of a very popular conception of learning, Bloom's taxonomy of learning. First proposed in 1956, Bloom's taxonomy lists the skills we should aim for our pupils to develop. Knowing is at the bottom. Further up the ladder are apply, analyse, compare and evaluate, which are all examples of higher-order thinking skills.[22]

It is arguable, and it has been argued, that this removal of content from the NC did not mean that teachers were not meant to teach content. It simply gave them more freedom over the content that they did choose. I do not accept this. When we consider the evidence I have outlined previously, we see that the aim of removing content from the curriculum was so that the teacher would teach less content. The point of the curriculum was to encourage activities and learning experiences that involved much less transmission of knowledge and much more of a focus on conceptual understanding. The new NC accepted the idea that the transmission of knowledge hindered conceptual understanding.

Why is it a myth?

My aim here is not to criticise true conceptual understanding, genuine appreciation of significance or higher-order skill development. All of these things are indeed the true aim of education. My argument is that facts and subject content are not opposed to such aims; instead, they are part of it. Rousseau, Dewey and Freire were wrong to see facts as the enemy of understanding. All the scientific research of the last half-century proves them wrong. The modern bureaucrats and educationalists who base policy and practice on their thinking are wrong too, and with less excuse, as they have been alive when evidence that refutes these ideas has been discovered. Rousseau was writing in the eighteenth century; Dewey at the turn of the twentieth; Freire in the 1970s. Research from the second half of the twentieth century tells us that their analyses of factual learning are based on fundamentally faulty premises.

Much of the modern research into human intelligence was inspired and informed by research into artificial intelligence. To construct a machine that could think, scientists needed a better understanding of how humans actually thought.[23] One of the pioneers in this field, Herbert Simon, gained much of his insight into how humans think through his attempts to construct a thinking machine.[24] In the 1960s and 1970s, researchers agreed on a basic mental model of cognition that has been refined and honed since then.[25] What this model shows is that the facts we have in long-term memory are vitally important for cognition. Kirschner and co-workers put it thus:

> Our understanding of the role of long-term memory in human cognition has altered dramatically over the last few decades. It is no longer seen as a passive repository of discrete, isolated fragments of information that permit us to repeat what we have learned. Nor is it seen only as a component of human cognitive architecture that has merely peripheral influence on complex cognitive processes such as thinking and problem solving. Rather, long-term memory is now viewed as the central, dominant structure of human cognition. Everything we see, hear, and think about is critically dependent on and influenced by our long-term memory.[26]

By understanding how the brain works, or what Kirschner and co-workers call human cognitive architecture, we can understand why this is so. When we encounter a problem we want to solve, we can use working memory and long-term memory to solve it. 'Working memory can be equated with consciousness. Humans are conscious of and can monitor only the contents of working memory. All other cognitive functioning is hidden from view unless and until it can be brought into working memory.'[27] So when we want to solve a problem, we hold all the information relating to the problem in working memory. Unfortunately, working memory is highly limited. There is some debate in the literature about exactly how limited working memory is, but some of the most recent research suggests that it may be limited to as few as three or four items.[28] That is, we can hold only three or four new items in working memory at any one time. This places a huge limit on our ability to solve problems. You can see this by increasing the length of a range of multiplication problems. If you are asked to solve the problem 46×7 mentally, then it is possible for you to succeed, because doing so does not require you to hold too much new information in your working memory at once. But there is still a chance you will make errors, because you do have to use your working memory to remember a few things. You can solve this problem in a couple of ways; the following two are probably the most common:

1   $6 \times 7 = 42$.
2   Put 2 down, carry 4.
3   $7 \times 4 = 28$.

4   Add 4 to 28 = 32.
5   Remember you had put 2 down = 322.

OR

1   7 × 40 = 280.
2   7 × 6 = 42.
3   280 + 42 = 322.

Whatever method you use to calculate this, you have to hold one piece of information in your working memory while you work out the next piece. Then you have to remember the first piece of information because you need to do something that involves using it and the second piece together. It is typical when solving problems like this to forget the result of the first calculation by the time you have got to the end of the last calculation. Multiplying a three-digit number by a one-digit number would test working memory even further.

And if you are asked to solve the problem 23,322 × 42 mentally, you almost certainly will not succeed. It is not that you do not know how to solve the problem; it is that solving it involves you holding far too many new pieces of information in your working memory at once.

Although working memory is limited, it is possible to cheat its constraints. Our long-term memory does not have the same limitations as working memory. It is capable of storing thousands of pieces of information. We can summon up the information from long-term memory to working memory without imposing a cognitive load. This allows us to cheat the limitations of working memory in lots of ways. For example, we can use the knowledge stored in long-term memory to chunk. If I present you with 16 digits that you have to look at for five seconds and then try to reproduce, you will probably fail:

4871947503858604

But if I present you with the following 16 letters for five seconds, you will probably be able to reproduce them all exactly:

The cat is on the mat.[29]

This is because you have been able to chunk the 16 letters into individual and meaningful words, and then into one individual phrase or sentence. That chunking is dependent on your background knowledge, stored in your long-term memory, of the way that letters form words, the meaning of each individual word and the typical structure of a sentence.

We can also store rules or processes in long-term memory. These help us to know how to solve a problem. The only reason it is possible for us to solve a problem like 46 × 7 mentally is that we have certain pieces of knowledge stored in memory which help us tackle the problem. We know that the process of multiplying a double-digit number with a single digit involves multiplying the units, carrying any ten, and then multiplying the unit with the ten. We also know that 7 × 3 = 21 and that 7 × 2 = 14. This problem involves a lot more than three pieces of information. But it is possible to solve it because most of us have the relevant knowledge in long-term memory. If you do not have the relevant knowledge securely committed to long-term memory, it becomes much more difficult. Pupils who have not committed the times tables to memory cannot solve a problem like that mentally, even if they understand conceptually how multiplication works.

So, when we commit facts to long-term memory, they actually become part of our thinking apparatus and have the ability to expand one of the biggest limitations of human cognition. Anderson puts it thus:

> All that there is to intelligence is the simple accrual and tuning of many small units of knowledge that in total produce complex cognition. The whole is no more than the sum of its parts, but it has a lot of parts.[30]

A lot is no exaggeration. Long-term memory is capable of storing thousands of facts, and when we have memorised thousands of facts on a specific topic, these facts together form what is known as a schema. When we think about that topic, we use that schema. When we meet new facts about that topic, we assimilate them into that schema – and if we already have a lot of facts in that particular schema, it is much easier for us to learn new facts about that topic.[31]

Critics of fact-learning will often pull out a completely random fact and say something like: who needs to know the date of the Battle of Waterloo? Why does it matter? Of course, pulling out one fact like this on its own does seem rather odd. But the aim of fact-learning is not to learn just one fact – it is to learn several hundred, which taken together form a schema that helps you to understand the world. Thus, just learning the date of the Battle of Waterloo will be of limited use. But learning the dates of 150 historical events from 3000 BC to the present day and learning a couple of key facts about why each event was important will be of immense use, because it will form the fundamental chronological schema that is the basis of all historical understanding. Just learning that 4 × 4 is 16 will be of limited use. But learning all of the 12 times tables, and learning them all so securely that we can hardly not think of the answer when the problem is presented, is the basis of mathematical understanding. If we want pupils to have good conceptual understanding, they need more facts, not fewer.

For Rousseau, Dewey, Freire and the writers of the NC, factual knowledge is seen as being in opposition to the kinds of abilities and thinking they want to develop. They all identify that teaching facts without meaning is unhelpful. But they all make a further assumption: that teaching facts is therefore opposed to teaching meaning. But this is not true. Factual knowledge is not in opposition to creativity, problem-solving and analysis, or indeed meaning and understanding. Factual knowledge is closely integrated with these important skills. It allows these skills to happen. In a sense, these important skills are the functions of large bodies of knowledge that have been securely committed to memory.

If we want pupils to develop the skills of analysis and evaluation, they need to know things. Dan Willingham puts it thus:

> Data from the last thirty years lead to a conclusion that is not scientifically challengeable: thinking well requires knowing facts, and that's true not just because you need something to think about. The very processes that teachers care about most – critical thinking processes such as reasoning and problem solving – are intimately intertwined with factual knowledge that is stored in long-term memory (not just found in the environment).[32]

As we have seen, the popular Bloom's taxonomy suggests that knowing is a lower-order skill, while analysing and evaluating are higher-order skills. The metaphor of lower and higher skills leads to two false conclusions. First, it suggests that the skills are somehow separate from knowledge. Second, it suggests that knowledge is somehow less worthy and important. A better metaphor than this lower/higher one is that used by E.D. Hirsch. He sees the relationship between knowledge and skills as being like a scrambled egg.[33] You cannot unscramble an egg, and you cannot unscramble knowledge and skills. I also like the metaphor suggested by my colleague Joe Kirby, that knowledge and skills are like a double helix, progressing in tandem from surface learning to deep learning. Rather than characterising passive fact-learning as surface, and active skill-practice as deep, we should understand that knowledge and skills are intertwined, and that skill progression depends upon knowledge accumulation.

I want to give a couple of practical examples of how this works. Perhaps the most fundamental example is learning the letters of the alphabet and the sounds they make. The letters of the alphabet are, in a sense, completely arbitrary. There is no good reason why the squiggle 'a' should form the vowel sound that we all do associate it with. Yet we accept that pupils have to learn the relationship between these arbitrary squiggles and sounds as a precursor to being able to make meaning from them. Learning such facts does not preclude meaning: it allows meaning. As the pupils commit these facts to memory, they are expanding their long-term memories, improving their ability to communicate and developing a more sophisticated mental apparatus.

A more sophisticated example comes from the education of Shakespeare, who we can all, I hope, agree was a particularly creative playwright:

> Shakespeare is an outstanding example of how schooling can foster talent. His education at Stratford-upon-Avon Grammar School gave him a

thorough grounding in the use of language and classical authors. Although his schooling might seem narrow and severe today (schoolboys learned by heart over 100 figures of rhetoric), it proved an excellent resource for the future playwright. Everything Shakespeare learned in school he used in some ways in his plays. At first, he applied his knowledge of the rules of language as he had acquired it at school. Some of his early plays seem to have a very obvious pattern and regular rhythm, almost mechanical and like clockwork. But having mastered the rules, he was able to break and transform them; to move from *Titus Andronicus* and *The Two Gentlemen of Verona* to *Hamlet* and *The Tempest*. On this evidence, Shakespeare's education has been seen as an argument for the value of learning by rote, of constant practice, of strict rule-following. Or, to put it another way, 'discovery favours the well-prepared mind'. Even the early plays show the same quality of writing that characterises his greatest plays. Shakespeare turned his school knowledge into striking dramatic action and vividly realised characters. His dramatic imagination was fuelled by what would now be seen as sterile exercises in memorisation and constant practice. What was mechanical became fluid, dramatic language that produced thrilling theatre.[34]

Of course, not everyone who had this education was capable of writing such brilliant plays. Shakespeare's creative genius was in the way he used the knowledge he had gained. But it is very clear from this analysis that a fact-filled education did *not* stifle that genius; on the contrary, this education allowed that genius to flourish.

By neglecting to focus on knowledge accumulation, therefore, and assuming that you can just focus on developing conceptual understanding, the NC ensures not only that pupils' knowledge will remain limited, but also that for all the apparent focus on conceptual understanding, their conceptual understanding will not develop either. By assuming that pupils can develop chronological awareness, write creatively or think like a scientist without learning any facts, we are guaranteeing that they will not develop any of those skills.

Consider what Dan Willingham has to say about such lessons. He recommends that when you require pupils to use higher-order skills, you ensure that the knowledge base is already in place:

> I once observed a teacher ask her fourth grade class what they thought it would be like to live in a rain forest. Although the students had spent a couple of days talking about rain forests, they didn't have the background knowledge to give anything beyond rather shallow responses (such as 'it would be rainy'). She asked the same question at the end of the unit, and the students' answers were much richer. One student immediately said that she wouldn't want to live there because the poor soil and constant

shade would mean she would probably have to include meat in her diet – and she was a vegetarian.[35]

This is another excellent example of how knowledge builds to allow sophisticated higher-order responses. You can only make that response if you *know* that rainforests have poor soil and constant shade, and if you *know* that this makes it difficult to grow agricultural crops there.

When the knowledge base is not in place, pupils struggle to develop understanding of a topic. I would often begin a new topic with a picture and a higher-order question. For example, I would start a lesson on Shakespeare with a picture of Shakespeare and the question 'What can you infer from this picture?' I would start a lesson on war poetry with a picture of a First World War trench and the question 'What do you think it would be like to live here?' My pupils always gave fairly unsophisticated and low-level answers. Answers to the latter question would often involve pupils saying 'horrible'. When I would prompt them to expand, they would say 'really horrible'. When I asked them why, they would say 'because there's lots of mud there, and I don't like mud'. Occasionally, a maverick pupil would express the view that they would quite like to live there, because they liked war and they liked playing the video game *Call of Duty*. Sometimes, these questions would cause more problems than they were worth. For example, a pupil once looked at a picture of Shakespeare and told her group that he was a famous writer who had made the film of *Oliver Twist*. They had all dutifully recorded it in their books before I could reach them on my journey around the classroom. A common response to the picture of any man from the past was that he was rich, posh or gay. I remember once questioning pupils as to why they had come to this conclusion, and asking them to use the word 'because' in their answers. I had been advised to do this whilst I was training. The hope was that the word 'because' would prompt pupils to be analytical. I got answers such as 'because his jacket is funny' and 'because he is wearing weird clothes'. Generic strategies such as 'try and use the word because' cannot make up for lack of knowledge. It is true that using the word 'because' is a feature of analytical answers, but that does not mean that requiring pupils to use the word 'because' will result in good analytical answers. Good analytical answers depend on a body of knowledge, not on abstract advice to use a certain word in your answer. Forcing pupils to use a certain word will not give pupils the knowledge they need to be analytical.

It might be argued at this point that while I am right to argue for the importance of facts, I am wrong about how they should be taught. That is, the only reason these questioning methods did not work in my hands is because I was not a skilful enough teacher or questioner to ensure that the pupils were able to learn the correct facts through these methods. A skilful teacher would be able to ensure their pupils learned important facts through these methods, and they would do so far more effectively than methods that are solely concerned with imparting facts.

While I am perfectly prepared to admit that I am not particularly skilled at these methods, I do not think this argument is quite fair. The rhetoric from these theorists and from the NC suggests that facts are unimportant and that we would do better to dwell on conceptual understanding, not that there are better and worse ways of imparting facts. The theorists and government agencies I have presented in this chapter are clearly sceptical about the value of facts *per se*. As we have seen, their rhetoric positions facts against understanding.

However, the question of method is still an important one. Because these theorists are sceptical about the value of facts, they are also sceptical about the value of teaching methods that aim to impart facts. In the next chapter, we will look at how these methods have been denigrated and attacked by influential theorists and by government agencies.

Notes

1 Rousseau, J.-J. *Emile, or Education*. Translated by Barbara Foxley. London: Dent, 1921, 1911, p. 56.
2 Ibid., p. 76.
3 Ibid., p. 72.
4 Ibid., p. 76.
5 Hickman, L.A. and Alexander, T.M. (eds). *The Essential Dewey. Volume 1, Pragmatism, Education, Democracy*. Bloomington: Indiana University Press, 1998, p. 233.
6 Ibid.
7 Pedagogy of the Oppressed. About Pedagogy of the Oppressed, www.pedagogyoftheoppressed.com/about/ (accessed 6 March 2013).
8 The Teacher (January–February 08). Best books (2008), p. 18, www.teachers.org.uk/files/teacher_feb08w.pdf (accessed 3 March 2013).
9 Freire, P. *Pedagogy of the Oppressed*. London: Penguin, 1996, p. 52.
10 Ibid., p. 53.
11 Dickens, C. *Hard Times*. London and New York: Penguin, 2003, p. 9.
12 Originally broadcast on 21 June 2012. Barely a month can go by without an article in the educational press mentioning Gradgrind. Here are a few selections from 2012: Garner, R. Back to basics: Will Gove's National Curriculum overhaul prepare children for the future? (2012), www.independent.co.uk/news/education/schools/back-to-basics-will-goves-national-curriculum-overhaul-prepare-children-for-the-future-7848765.html (accessed 3 March 2013); Penny, L. To hell with the Gradgrinds – go to university (2012), www.independent.co.uk/voices/commentators/laurie-penny-to-hell-with-the-gradgrinds-go-to-university-8050313.html (accessed 3 March 2013); Deary, T. History is about people, not 1066 and all that (2012), www.telegraph.co.uk/news/politics/david-cameron/9570845/History-is-about-people-not-1066-and-all-that.html (accessed 3 March 2013); Jenkins, S. Michael Gove's centralism is not so much socialist as Soviet (2012), www.guardian.co.uk/commentisfree/2012/oct/11/michael-gove-more-soviet-than-socialist (accessed 3 March 2013).

13 UNICEF Innocenti Research Centre (Report Card 7). Child poverty in perspective: An overview of child well-being in rich countries. A comprehensive assessment of the lives and well-being of children and adolescents in the economically advanced nations (2007), www.unicef.org/media/files/ChildPovertyReport.pdf (accessed 3 March 2013); Ipsos MORI Social Research Institute and Nairn, A. Children's well-being in UK, Sweden and Spain: The role of inequality and materialism (2011), www.unicef.org.uk/Documents/Publications/IPSOS_UNICEF_Child WellBeingreport.pdf (accessed 3 March 2013).

14 Qualifications and Curriculum Authority. *The National Curriculum.* London: Qualifications and Curriculum Authority, 2007, p. 114.

15 Ibid., p. 209.

16 Qualifications and Curriculum Authority. The new secondary curriculum: What has changed and why (2007), p. 4, http://dera.ioe.ac.uk/6564/1/qca-07-3172-new_sec_curric_changes.pdf (accessed 3 March 2013).

17 Qualifications and Curriculum Authority. Intended outcomes of the secondary curriculum (2013), http://webarchive.nationalarchives.gov.uk/20100823130703/http://curriculum.qcda.gov.uk/key-stages-3-and-4/About-the-secondary-curriculum/Intended-outcomes/index.aspx (accessed 3 March 2013).

18 Qualifications and Curriculum Authority. The new secondary curriculum: What has changed and why (2007), p. 2, http://dera.ioe.ac.uk/6564/1/qca-07-3172-new_sec_curric_changes.pdf (accessed 3 March 2013).

19 Wilby, P. Mick Waters, curriculum guru, takes stock. *Guardian* (2010), www.guardian.co.uk/education/2010/sep/07/mick-waters-qualifications-curriculum-authority (accessed 3 March 2013).

20 Johnson, M. *Subject to Change: New Thinking on the Curriculum.* London: ATL, 2007.

21 Association of Teachers and Lecturers. No silver bullet (2012), www.atl.org.uk/publications-and-resources/report/2012/2012-march-no-silver-bullet.asp (accessed 3 March 2013).

22 Bloom, B.S. *Taxonomy of Educational Objectives: The Classification of Educational Goals. Handbook I: Cognitive Domain.* New York: Longman, 1956, pp. 201–207.

23 McCorduck, P. *Machines Who Think: A Personal Inquiry into the History and Prospects of Artificial Intelligence.* 2nd edn. Natick: AK Peters, 2004.

24 Frantz, R. Herbert Simon. Artificial intelligence as a framework for understanding intuition. *Journal of Economic Psychology* 2003; 24: 265–277.

25 See, for example: Rumelhart, D.E. and Ortony, A. The representation of knowledge in memory. In: Anderson, R.C., Spiro, R.J. and Montague, W.E. (eds) *Schooling and the Acquisition of Knowledge.* Hillsdale: Lawrence Erlbaum Associates, 1977; Anderson, R.C. and Pearson, P.D. A schema-theoretic view of basic processes in reading comprehension. In: Pearson, P.D. (ed.) *Handbook of Reading Research.* New York: Longman, 1984, pp. 255–291; Atkinson, R. and Shiffrin, R. Human memory: A proposed system and its control processes. In: Spence, K.W. and Spence, J.T. (eds) *The Psychology of Learning and Motivation: Advances in Theory and Research. Volume 2.* New York: Academic Press, 1968, pp. 89–195; Ericsson, K.A. and Kintsch, W. Long-term working memory. *Psychological Review* 1995; 102: 211–245; Baddeley, A. *Working Memory, Thought and Action.* London: Oxford University Press, 2007.

26 Kirschner, P.A., Sweller, J. and Clark, R.E. Why minimal guidance during instruction does not work: An analysis of the failure of constructivist, discovery, problem-based, experiential, and inquiry-based teaching. *Educational Psychologist* 2006; 41: 75–86.

27 Sweller, J., van Merriënboer, J.J.G. and Paas, F.G.W.C. Cognitive architecture and instructional design. *Educational Psychology Review* 1998; 10: 251–296.

28 Cowan, N. The magical number 4 in short-term memory: A reconsideration of mental storage capacity. *Behavioral and Brain Sciences* 2001; 24: 87–114; Cowan, N. *Working Memory Capacity: Essays in Cognitive Psychology*. Hove: Psychology Press, 2005. See also Miller, G.A. The magical number seven, plus or minus two: Some limits on our capacity for processing information. *Psychological Review* 1956; 63: 81–97.

29 These examples are adapted from Hirsch, E.D. *Cultural Literacy: What Every American Needs to Know*. Boston: Houghton Mifflin, 1987, pp. 34–35.

30 Anderson, J.R. ACT: A simple theory of complex cognition. *American Psychologist* 1996; 51: 355–365.

31 Johnson Laird, P.N. *Mental Models: Towards a Cognitive Science of Language, Inference and Consciousness*. Cambridge, MA: Harvard University Press, 1983; Anderson, R.C. and Pearson, P.D. A schema-theoretic view of basic processes in reading comprehension. In: Pearson, P.D. (ed.) *Handbook of Reading Research*. New York: Longman, 1984, pp. 255–291.

32 Willingham, D.T. *Why Don't Students Like School?* San Francisco: Jossey-Bass, 2009, p. 28.

33 Hirsch, E.D. The 21st century skills movement. *Common Core News* (2011), http://commoncore.org/pressrelease-04.php (accessed 3 March 2013).

34 Gibson, R. *Teaching Shakespeare*. Cambridge: Cambridge University Press, 1998, pp. 46–47.

35 Willingham, D.T. *Why Don't Students Like School?* San Francisco: Jossey-Bass, 2009, pp. 48–49.

Myth 2

Teacher-led instruction is passive

Where is the evidence that people believe this and that it has affected education policy and classroom practice?

Theoretical evidence

In the last chapter we saw how many theorists of education were highly sceptical of the value of facts in education. I finished the chapter by suggesting the possibility that they were not sceptical of facts, just of certain methods of imparting facts. And certainly, many of these theorists are very hostile towards certain teacher-directed methods of learning facts, which are seen as passive and dehumanising. They argue that because such methods are passive and dehumanising, they are actually ultimately ineffective at teaching the facts. It is not just more moral but more effective for pupils to learn all the facts they do need through a process that involves much less teacher guidance. If the teacher designs a learning environment well enough, pupils will be able to learn with minimal guidance or through discovery.

Here is Rousseau criticising the value of the teacher questioning the pupil:

> Too many questions are tedious and revolting to most of us and especially to children. After a few minutes their attention flags, they cease to listen to your everlasting questions and reply at random. This way of testing them is pedantic and useless.[1]

For Rousseau, you should not even formally teach a child to read by explaining the alphabet and the sounds the letters make. Instead, by carefully designing a learning environment, you should aim to stimulate the child's curiosity so that they will pick up whatever is important:

> Present interest, that is the motive power, the only motive power that takes us far and safely. Sometimes Émile receives notes of invitation from his father or mother, his relations or friends; he is invited to a dinner, a walk, a boating expedition, to see some public entertainment. These notes are short, clear, plain, and well written. Some one must read them to him, and

he cannot always find anybody when wanted ... Time passes, the chance is lost. The note is read to him at last, but it is too late. Oh! if only he had known how to read! He receives other notes, so short, so interesting, he would like to try to read them. Sometimes he gets help, sometimes none. He does his best, and at last he makes out half the note; it is something about going to-morrow to drink cream—Where? With whom? He cannot tell—how hard he tries to make out the rest! I do not think Émile will need a 'bureau'. [Translator's note: The 'bureau' was a sort of case containing letters to be put together to form words. It was a favourite device for the teaching of reading and gave its name to a special method, called the bureau-method, of learning to read.] Shall I proceed to the teaching of writing? No, I am ashamed to toy with these trifles in a treatise on education.[2]

Dewey also praised methods where the child's own inclinations and interests were allowed to determine the education process:

I believe, therefore, that the true centre of correlation of the school subjects is not science, nor literature, nor history, nor geography, but the child's own social activities.[3]

We saw in the previous chapter how Freire criticised the banking concept of education, where facts prevented true understanding. Freire also puts forward an alternative version of education, one that is based around discussion, dialogue and enquiry. Rather than the teacher transmitting knowledge to the pupil, the discussion and dialogue between the teacher and student would result in the creation of new knowledge. This should be the aim of education, and it has come to be known as the co-construction of knowledge:

For apart from inquiry, apart from the praxis, individuals cannot be truly human. Knowledge emerges only through invention and re-invention, through the restless, impatient continuing, hopeful inquiry human beings pursue in the world, with the world, and with each other.[4]

The teacher should no longer be a figure of authority, but should instead become a student among students:

Education must begin with the solution of the teacher-student contradiction, by reconciling the poles of the contradiction so that both are simultaneously teachers and students.[5]

A Freirean practitioner gives a more concrete example of how this approach works:

Freire translated his theoretical analysis into a practical methodology. The key step was to enable people to reflect on their lives. To achieve this, Freire developed 'codifications' – pictures or photographs which capture essential contradictions in the local environment. Through dialogue, participants 'decode' these, slowly confronting their reality. The pictures are then related to resonant 'generative words' which are used to introduce reading and writing.[6]

Drill and memorisation are also frequently criticised by these theorists, and many modern writers apply the pejorative phrases 'rote learning' and 'drill and kill' to such practices.[7] Rousseau tells us that 'Emile will not learn anything by heart'.[8] Freire criticises practice that involves pupils memorising facts, because such memorisation stops them from understanding the true meaning of things:

> Words are emptied of their concreteness and become a hollow, alienated, and alienating verbosity … 'Four times four is sixteen; the capital of Para is Belem.' The student records, memorises, and repeats these phrases without perceiving what four times four really means, or realising the true significance of 'capital' in the affirmation 'the capital of Para is Belem,' that is, what Belem means for Para and what Para means for Brazil.[9]

To listen to these educationalists, teaching facts is bad for two reasons. First, it is actually immoral. It damages the child. It knocks all the joy and spontaneity out of childhood and turns the child into a passive and unthinking creature. Second, it is ineffective. It does not work. Teaching facts will not actually help pupils learn. They will just have remembered a lot of things that have no meaning to them. They will not really be thinking; they will just be regurgitating. There are many more effective ways you can educate pupils, ways that are both more effective and more joyful. Instead of learning external facts in a formal manner, pupils should learn through minimal guidance and discovery. The phrase often associated with these different, less teacher-directed methods of teaching is that the teacher should be the 'guide on the side', rather than the 'sage on the stage'.[10]

Modern practice

Again, the assumption of many people would be that there is too much teacher-led learning in English classrooms, and that one of the reasons for this is because Ofsted require such teaching. Dr Peter Ovens, an academic from the University of Cumbria, published research suggesting that 'around a third of university students struggled to learn independently'.[11] He argued that this was the result of school teaching that had been too focused on 'meeting targets and Ofsted requirements'.[12] He concluded with a Gradgrindian metaphor, arguing that 'academics should not view students as empty vessels to be filled with knowledge'.[13] In this argument, the reason why students fail to learn independently is because they have been led through their schooling by teachers who are focused on Ofsted requirements. But what I want to show here is that the practice is very different from this. Teachers are indeed focused on meeting Ofsted requirements, but those requirements do not encourage them to lead the teaching in their classroom. On the contrary, Ofsted require teachers to give children the control of the classroom, just as Dewey, Rousseau and Freire suggest. In this chapter, I want to look closely at the advice Ofsted give to teachers. In Chapter 1, we looked at the National Curriculum's (NC) conception of learning and facts, but for evidence of how this curriculum actually works in the classroom, Ofsted provide the most reliable evidence.

First of all, we need to prove the reliability and significance of these Ofsted lessons. As with the NC, there is a statutory requirement for Ofsted to inspect schools in England. Ofsted inspectors will observe lessons and judge them, as well as inspecting a school's systems and leadership. If Ofsted judge a school to be failing, it can lead to the dismissal of the head and even the closure of the school. If Ofsted observe an individual teacher's lesson and judge it to be unsatisfactory, that can have severe ramifications for that teacher's career. The amount of pressure that teachers and managers feel when being inspected by Ofsted is well-documented.[14] Ofsted quite clearly have significant powers. Working out what Ofsted want is practically a cottage industry, with consultants, bloggers and advisers all competing to explain to schools exactly what they need to do to get the coveted outstanding grade.[15]

Ofsted publish the criteria for lesson observations online. The criteria for lesson observations have recently been changed, but both the old and new versions are rather vague. A lot depends on the interpretation of certain phrases, which is why I want to consider other Ofsted publications. As well as the lesson observation criteria, Ofsted also publish their inspection reports of individual schools. These reports offer more concrete explanations of what makes a good lesson than the criteria do, but they still do not describe classroom practice in very close detail. The most useful type of publication for our purposes are their subject reports. In these reports, inspectors select the very best practice they have seen in their subject across all the thousands of lessons they have collectively observed. In using these reports, I am not suggesting that every single teacher in the country has read their subject's report in close detail (although I think that some doubtless have, and I have attended internal and external training where these reports have been discussed at length). I am suggesting that nearly every teacher in the country is closely attuned to what Ofsted want, and that these lesson descriptions give us the most reliable way of working out what it is Ofsted want. From my experience in teaching, I think that these lesson descriptions do closely correspond to what Ofsted want. One of the strongest messages I received when I was training and beginning to teach was that I should not talk very much. I remember one teacher trainer telling me that if I was talking, the pupils were not learning. After my first Ofsted inspection, the inspector praised my lesson for the way that in the plan and in practice, I had kept the time I spent talking to a minimum. By looking at the subject reports, we can see that this type of advice and praise is not unusual.

The one flaw with these reports is that Ofsted inspections are pre-announced. This means that teachers can, and do, put on a show for Ofsted. It has long been a complaint of many teachers that the kind of lesson Ofsted grade as outstanding is simply not possible to repeat consistently. So, when I give an example of an outstanding lesson from an Ofsted report, I do not mean to suggest that lessons exactly like this are going on all the time. However, given the power we have seen Ofsted have, given the cottage industry of Ofsted preparation and given the fact that most schools will organise their own internal observation systems around Ofsted criteria, it is still fair to say that if Ofsted demand a certain type of lesson, that matters. Teachers will hear about it and they will take heed. So, Ofsted's inspection reports and subject reports are a fairly reliable guide to what actually happens in schools and a very reliable guide to what teachers are told to do.

Having established the significance of Ofsted, what exactly is it that they demand? The publications of Ofsted consistently promote one key message that is clearly influenced by the theoretical ideas I have outlined previously. In the broadest terms, they warn the teacher against giving too much direction. Teachers are warned not to talk too much and not to tell pupils things. They are encouraged to plan lessons where pupils discuss something they already know or where pupils find things out for themselves, often in groups of peers.

In the Appendix to this book, which is available online, I have summarised all the concrete examples of lessons in subject reports from the following subjects: art, English, geography, history, maths, modern foreign languages (MFL), religious education (RE) and science.[16] Most of these lessons are examples of what Ofsted consider to be good or outstanding; only a few contain examples of bad teaching. In total, there are 228 lessons, broken down as follows: art (26), English (33), geography (42), history (18), maths (18), MFL (54), RE (19) and science (18). These reports are recent: the oldest is from June 2010 and the most recent from May 2012.[17]

I think that some of the lessons Ofsted praise are very bad lessons, and I shall go on to explain why later in this chapter and in Chapters 5 and 6. But for now, my point is not about whether these lessons are good or bad; for now, my point is that, of the lessons that are praised, very few involve the teacher teaching facts. In the lessons that are criticised, very often the feature being criticised is the teacher talking too much, or imparting facts or teaching activities that involve factual recall. Here are just a few examples of such lessons.

In this English lesson, instead of the teacher explaining new knowledge to the pupils, the pupils discuss something that they know already:

A group of more able students was producing a school radio programme. The students had decided to create a soap opera, using a range of characters to explore issues of interest to a teenage audience. It was to be presented as part of the daily broadcasts for students. The inspector observed a writers' meeting, where students (supported by the teacher) worked on a script for one of the programmes. An earlier version of the script had been presented to members of the school's pastoral team who had suggested changes. As a result, members of the writing team worked closely together to introduce some new elements to the script. The meeting was a remarkably successful and realistic one, taking on all the elements of the kind of writers' meeting that you might get as part of a real TV or radio soap opera. One of the students described it as 'creative writing mixed with reality'. There was a very open discussion, with students making suggestions and editing as they worked. The inspector noted that the normal roles of teacher and learner appeared to have merged.[18]

This merging of the roles of teacher and learner is something that Freire recommended.

Another English example involves pupils writing about something they already know about, thus removing the need for the teacher to transmit knowledge:

> One simple example was work in Year 7 on a letter to the headteacher about school uniform. This was followed by a visit by the headteacher to discuss the issues with the class.[19]

Even when pupils are being introduced to something they do not know, often the focus is still on their discussion and ideas, and the teacher's input is still limited. In this example of a lesson about angels from an RE subject report, teacher direction is limited to setting up the task. There is no transmission of knowledge from teacher to pupil. There is discussion among pupils and the teacher only facilitates the discussion and records the answers at the end:

> The teacher focused the enquiry by explaining to the pupils that they were on a quest for angels and asking them what thoughts and questions came to their minds when they heard the word 'angels'. They were then given a number of questions to discuss in groups including: 'What might/do angels look like?'; 'What is their job?'; 'Are they real or imaginary?'; 'Are they like fairies?' 'What would you do if you met an angel?'; 'What difference could an angel make?' The outcomes were shared and recorded.[20]

When lessons do involve pupils being introduced to new knowledge, often it is not teachers directing them to new knowledge, but their own interests and inclinations, as in this English lesson:

> Pupils are put into mixed-ability groups and given an assortment of journals and newspapers to trawl through. They select an item that interests them – any item – and put together a brief presentation about its content for the plenary session.[21]

Even when a lesson does involve some knowledge that the pupils do not already know, there is rarely any time given over for the teacher to explain this knowledge. In these reports, sentences rarely begin with 'the teacher explains' but more often with 'the pupils discuss'. For example, in a geography lesson that involved preparing for a field trip, teachers did not tell pupils about the health and safety rules or explain them. Instead, pupils discussed them:

> Year 3/4 pupils completed field observations with the teacher and teaching assistant. Discussion had taken place about health and safety and care of equipment as pupils moved from the classroom to practical activities.[22]

In these lessons, it is often quite hard to work out what the teacher is doing. Lessons are described where it seems that pupils – even very young pupils – are doing most of the planning and teaching of lessons. In these lessons, the teacher is often not even mentioned. Here is a lesson from the science report where all of the planning and activities seem to be determined by the pupils:

> Year 8 students were completing a unit of work on acids and alkalis that had involved them in research on the effect of acid rain on limestone. They had worked in groups to generate their own questions to pursue. Many of them had taken the time to form hypotheses and had planned and carried out their own practical work. The students had presented the outcomes of their research to the class in the form of high-quality PowerPoint presentations. Discussion with the students showed how varied these presentations were.[23]

Here is a geography lesson where an even younger group of pupils run the lesson:

> Year 4 pupils used drama to consider the impact of loggers and tourists on the native population of the Brazilian rainforest. Small groups of pupils presented their cameos and the others listened carefully to the viewpoints.[24]

There are other examples of lessons where the pupils are praised for having knowledge, but where the teaching of the knowledge is still never shown. This is particularly prominent in the MFL report. This report praises pupils who have solid understanding of grammatical techniques, but it never shows pupils in the process of learning those techniques:

> A good example of pupils showing understanding of sound spelling links occurred when two Year 4 boys wrote 'un chat blue' on their mini whiteboards and read it out to each other. They immediately realised that they could not pronounce 'blue' as 'bleu' and that they had used the English spelling. They quickly corrected their work. In this class pupils

instantly took to spelling in French, and were conversant with how the alphabet sounds in French.[25]

So here, instead of the Ofsted inspectors explaining and praising the way teachers teach pupils to spell in French, they praise the way pupils spontaneously 'took to spelling in French'.[26]

Most of these reports focus on describing good practice, but they also give a few examples of bad practice. In the art subject report, there are descriptions of 26 lessons or learning experiences; 24 are entirely positive. Here is one lesson that is criticised:

> Following discussion about the meaning of 'abstract' and 'expressionism' definitions were provided by the teacher and glued into sketchbooks. A biographical summary of Frank Stella's life was also provided. This reading was followed by questions focused on students' recall of factual information. Laminated images of Stella's work were used to stimulate the practical activity that followed.[27]

This lesson is criticised because it is 'overly dependent on students' literacy skills' and because 'opportunities were missed to engage students fully in their learning'.[28] It is the only lesson in the report that explicitly involves the teacher transmitting facts. Instead, the art report praises lessons that involve much more informal exploration and learning:

> First, children explored the concept of traditional weddings in different cultures. This included: dressing up; acting out make-believe ceremonies; painting pictures of brides and grooms; making wedding paraphernalia; writing lists and table place names; and making cakes, wedding gifts and trinkets. Staff identified two children who repeatedly headed straight to the activities to immerse themselves in creative play. They were chosen as 'bride' and 'groom' to re-enact a traditional Christian ceremony at the nearby local church. The children sent out invitations to family guests and members of the local community who came to witness the marriage. The local vicar presided over the ceremony and awarded an 'official' wedding certificate to the happy couple. Afterwards the children led their guests back to school for the wedding reception. Marquees were adorned with decorations and foods including the three-tier wedding cake the children had made previously. Fizzy drinks were used to toast the bride and groom and mark the special occasion. Digital photographs by the 'wedding photographer' captured the moment and children later recorded the day's events in paintings. An exhibition of their work displayed in the school hall prompted much interest and discussion among the community and visitors.[29]

Likewise, the RE report criticises lessons that 'tended to focus on gathering information rather than on developing pupils' skills of investigation, interpretation, analysis, evaluation and reflection'.[30] This is very similar to the opposition Dewey, Rousseau and Freire draw between facts and understanding.

The maths report also criticises lessons which involve teacher talk. It says that 'a feature of much of the satisfactory teaching was that teachers tended to talk for too long'.[31] (It is important to note that for Ofsted, satisfactory actually means 'requires improvement'.)[32] Instead, it praises lessons where explanations are kept 'suitably brief'.[33] The following model of lesson, involving practice and factual recall, is criticised:

> A common feature of the satisfactory teaching observed was the use of examples followed by practice with many similar questions. This allowed consolidation of a skill or technique but did not develop problem-solving skills or understanding of concepts. The teachers typically demonstrated a standard method, giving tips to pupils on how to avoid making mistakes and, sometimes, 'rules' and mnemonics to help them commit the methods to memory. Many of their questions concerned factual recall so that pupils' 'explanations' often consisted of restating the method rather than justifying their answers.[34]

Lessons involving pupil-directed problem-solving are praised as an alternative:

> Pupils first matched each of the diverse group of party guests (baby mice through to a giant) to various balloons. Then they had to measure string of differing lengths (5cm to 2m) for tying onto the balloons for each guest. The higher level teaching assistant encouraged good debate between the pupils around whether the string should be measured and cut before tying, or tied first and then measured. She did not steer them towards the other approach when they decided to measure and tie the string first. The pupils wrestled with measuring the string after tying it to the balloons which enabled them to appreciate the difficulty of measuring accurately once the string was attached to the balloon. They also realised that some of the string was used up in tying it to the balloon. This led to good discussion around which approach should be taken. The pupils revised their strategy for the task, which they went on to complete successfully.[35]

For Ofsted, therefore, teacher-led fact-learning is highly problematic. In the rhetoric they use and the practical examples they give, we see that they largely subscribe to the theoretical view I outlined at the start of this chapter: that teaching a child facts that they have not encountered before makes the child passive and does not help to educate them. The alternatives they promote involve very little learning of facts, and very much more time spent discussing issues with limited teacher involvement.

Why is this a myth?

How true is this? Is it possible for pupils to independently learn all the facts they will need through well-designed learning experiences that involve minimal teacher instruction or talk? It is not. These arguments gain plausibility through a fundamental logical error. They argue, correctly, that the aim of schooling should be for pupils to be able to work, learn and solve problems independently. But they then assume, incorrectly, that the best method for achieving such independence is always to learn independently. This is not the case. Teacher instruction is vitally necessary to become an independent learner.

The first piece of evidence in favour of teacher instruction is historical. There are some abilities that we will just acquire naturally. For example, if young children are exposed to a spoken language, they will acquire the ability to speak that language and to understand it when it is spoken. That is how we all learn to speak and understand our mother tongue. We naturally acquire it. But many of the other essential things we want pupils to learn are not natural. The alphabet and the numbering system, which one would hope everyone would agree are essential parts of schooling, are both highly complex and abstract inventions of civilisation.[36] There is nothing natural about them. There was nothing inevitable about their invention, and there is nothing inevitable about young children discovering how they work, even if they are exposed to them. It is important to note, therefore, that while speaking and listening are natural, reading and writing, which seem so similar, are not at all natural. If children are exposed to language, they will learn how to speak it and understand it; if they are exposed to printed material, they will not necessarily learn how to read, write, spell and use punctuation correctly. These concepts require formal and explicit teaching.

The same is true of important scientific discoveries. In many cases, important scientific principles were first discovered through experience or exposure, but the people doing the discoveries were geniuses with exceptional insight. Newton may have developed his theory of gravitation when observing how apples always fall straight to the ground; however, apples had fallen straight to the ground for time immemorial without anyone else having Newton's breakthrough. The Greeks were taking baths for centuries before Archimedes worked out that an object that is wholly or partially immersed in a fluid is buoyed up by a force equal to the weight of the fluid displaced by the object. Once these breakthroughs are made, then we are all able to understand and use them, *if* they are explained to us. If they are not explained to us and we are left to discover them for ourselves, many people will simply never discover them, or will have very imperfect understandings of them. Even those pupils who do manage to learn through these methods will have taken a highly inefficient method that will have wasted a lot of time. Even Jerome Bruner, who was a fan of discovery learning, accepted this:

You cannot consider education without taking into account how culture gets passed on. It seems to me highly unlikely that given the centrality of culture in man's adaptation to his environment – the fact that culture serves him in the same way as changes in morphology served earlier in the evolutionary scale – that, biologically speaking, one would expect each organism to rediscover the totality of its culture – this would seem most unlikely. Moreover, it seems equally unlikely, given the nature of man's dependency as a creature, that this long period of dependency characteristic of our species was designed entirely for the most inefficient technique possible for regaining what has been gathered over a long period of time, i.e. discovery.[37]

In practice, we can see this is the case with the lessons recommended by Ofsted. The only way for independent learning to be practicable is for pupils to work with knowledge they already know; that is, to write letters about school uniforms or their local area. As a method for 'regaining what has been gathered over a long period of time', independent learning is ineffective. This is why so few of the lessons Ofsted praise involve pupils learning facts about classic literature, grammar, science, history and geography beyond the school gate. Thus, the claim that pupils can learn everything they need independently only holds true if we define everything they need so that it does not include any of the unnatural breakthroughs of civilisation: the alphabet, the numbering system, the principles that govern the natural world. To take a more mundane example, it means that pupils will find it difficult to learn rules about 'health and safety and care of equipment'.[38] Health and safety rules have been compiled through the trial and error of many humans – often very painful trial and error. To suggest that a year 3 class will work out all the important health and safety rules they need to know because a 'discussion had taken place' is highly optimistic and highly risky.[39] As Newton said, we learn by standing on the shoulders of giants.[40] If humanity has worked out through trial and error that a certain practice is dangerous and should be avoided, it is much safer and more efficient to be told that than to be left to discuss it among other novices. When carrying out any kind of fieldwork or experiment, it would seem sensible for the teacher to tell the children the possible dangers, explain why they are dangers and check they have understood. But this would not suit the demand for independent learning.

What we can also see from this is that Ofsted do not just object to teachers telling pupils facts. They even object to teachers explaining those facts. Freire criticised teachers who force their pupils to chant facts they do not understand; however, he does not conclude from this that teachers should explain to their pupils the meaning of four times four and the significance of capitals as well as helping them to memorise such facts. He concludes instead that there should be no memorising at all and that there should be no teacher explanation either. Ofsted reach the same conclusion, and they have not even encountered the bad practice Freire saw. It is a baffling overreaction: to move from legitimate criticism of mindless rote learning to the complete denial of any kind of teacher-led activity. The solution to mindless rote learning is not less teacher instruction; it is different and better teacher instruction.

There is one other point that needs to be made. Independent learning suggests a reduced and sometimes even non-existent role for the teacher. If it really were possible to learn independently, why would we need teachers and schools? It is no coincidence that many of the keenest advocates of independent learning did indeed want to abolish schools. Rousseau's advice has influenced generations of teachers, but actually he advocated homeschooling and rejected the formal setting of school. Another prominent advocate of such learning is Ivan Ilich.[41] He was also highly critical of the very concept of schools and teachers.

It is baffling that the English schools inspectorate should endorse such an anti-school and anti-teacher attitude. This is particularly the case in the MFL lessons they describe. In nearly all of these lessons, pupils are praised for knowing things and doing things spontaneously. The methods used to teach them are never mentioned; indeed, the impression we get is that they were never taught. Pupils are praised because they 'took to spelling in French'.[42] If it really were the case that they took spontaneously to spelling in French, why would such pupils need a school or teacher? If, as I suspect, their ability to spell in French is actually down to teacher instruction and explanation that happened prior to the Ofsted inspection, then such descriptions are highly misleading and even dangerous. They suggest to the teacher that if their pupil does not spontaneously pick up French spelling, the pupil is a failure. In fact, it is the teaching method – or rather, the absence of a teaching method – which is to blame.

The second piece of evidence in favour of teacher instruction is theoretical. There is a reason why it took humans such a long time to discover the laws of nature, even though the evidence for such laws was all around them in the environment. We do not find it easy to learn new information when we have no or minimal guidance. This is because of the limitations of working memory we saw in the previous chapter. When we are presented with lots of new information and very little guidance, it is hard for our working memories to make sense of all the new information. Because we are so busy finding ways to work with the new information, or searching for ways to make sense of it, we find it hard to commit the new information to memory:

> Inquiry-based instruction requires the learner to search a problem space for problem-relevant information. All problem-based searching makes heavy demands on working memory. Furthermore, that working memory load does not contribute to the accumulation of knowledge in long-term memory because while working memory is being used to search for problem solutions, it is not available and cannot be used to learn.[43]

Presenting pupils with complex problems and getting them to try to work out the answers on their own is not a good way for pupils to learn facts:

> Controlled experiments almost uniformly indicate that when dealing with novel information, learners should be explicitly shown what to do and how to do it.[44]

Nor is this approach a good way for pupils to develop proficiency at problem-solving:

> When students learn science in classrooms with pure-discovery methods and minimal feedback, they often become lost and frustrated, and their confusion can lead to misconceptions.[45]

Pupils will struggle to commit any facts to long-term memory while they are trying to make sense of lots of information on their own. What Kirschner, Sweller and Clark also tell us here is that they will struggle to solve the problem if they do not already have relevant bodies of knowledge. This kind of activity is meaningful if you already have knowledge. If you do not, you will likely get confused and frustrated as your working memory is overloaded. It is then very likely that you will give up.

This approach might be more suitable for pupils who already have extensive knowledge of a topic. But if they have always been taught via this method, it is unlikely they will have extensive knowledge of the topic. Pupils will be caught in a chicken-and-egg scenario: unable to work independently because they do not have the necessary background knowledge, but unable to gain that background knowledge because they spend all of their time working independently. New information combined with minimal guidance does not lead to effective learning. Instead, it leads to confusion, frustration and misconceptions. While the final aim of education is for our pupils to be able to work independently, endlessly asking them to work independently is not an effective method for achieving this aim. I shall consider this issue in more detail in Chapter 6 when I look at some popular and minimally guided projects and activities.

The third piece of evidence in favour of teacher instruction is empirical. The historical and theoretical evidence presented has been amply borne out by empirical evidence which shows that guided, teacher-led instruction is one of the most effective teaching methods. In his book *Visible Learning: A Synthesis of Over 800 Meta-Analyses Relating to Achievement*, the researcher John Hattie evaluates the success of a range of different teaching approaches. As the subtitle suggests, he synthesised the results of hundreds of different analyses of achievement and measured the effect of different factors. Direct teacher instruction was the third most powerful teacher factor. The only two more powerful teacher factors were feedback, which is not opposed to direct instruction and indeed is a part of it, and instructional quality, which again is not in opposition to direct instruction. Hattie defines direct instruction as follows:

> In a nutshell: The teacher decides the learning intentions and success criteria, makes them transparent to the students, demonstrates them by modelling, evaluates if they understand what they have been told by checking for understanding, and re-telling them what they have told by tying it all together with closure.[46]

A specific Direct Instruction programme was developed by the American educator, Siegfried Engelmann, in the 1960s. It proved incredibly successful but also incredibly controversial because it contradicted so much of what theorists like Dewey and Freire advocated. Hattie specifically endorsed Engelmann's programme, saying that 'the underlying principles of Direct Instruction place it among the most successful outcomes'.[47] Interestingly, Hattie also says that when he tells teacher trainees about this, they are shocked:

> Every year I present lectures to teacher education students and find that they are already indoctrinated with the mantra 'constructivism good, direct instruction bad'. When I show them the results of these meta-analyses, they are stunned, and they often become angry at having been given an agreed set of truths and commandments against direct instruction.[48]

I had a similar reaction to Hattie's pupils when I read his research. How could this be the case? Ofsted had been telling me over and over that I needed to talk less and get the pupils to be more independent. And yet one of the most respected researchers in the field was telling me that a highly formalised, explicit and teacher-led method of instruction was incredibly successful. Not one of the lessons praised by Ofsted in their subject reports could be classified as using direct instruction. In lessons that were criticised, such as the art lesson on expressionism, or the maths lesson involving practice, often it was the methods of direct instruction that were being criticised.

I planned and taught a sequence of lessons on English grammar based on the ideas of direct instruction. I was astonished at how successful they were. Pupils were able to learn concepts which I had previously thought were just too tricky or difficult for them to bother with. Not only that, they seemed to quite enjoy the lessons, too. In comparison to the independent learning approach I had used before, it was much more successful. I had taught similar lessons to the ones Ofsted recommended, where the pupils would work on their own scripts or write a letter to their headteacher about the school uniform. This approach to teaching clear and coherent writing asked pupils to fulfil an aim without actually teaching them how to do it. By using direct instruction and drill, I broke down the knowledge required to be a clear and coherent writer, sequenced it logically and taught each bit in isolation. I then asked students to practise it repeatedly. Whenever they learned a new piece of knowledge, I would ask them to practise that and to practise combining it with what they had learned before. This approach is effective because it means working memory is not overloaded. Pupils are able to learn and practise each piece of knowledge in isolation. There is not one lesson in the Ofsted exemplar English lessons that involves teaching grammar in this way. All the lessons on writing involve pupils doing extended writing. This approach requires good understanding of grammar, but does not teach that understanding. It just expects pupils will pick it up through exposure. But as we have seen, that is not realistic.

An argument levelled against this approach is that it is boring and demotivating. Of course, in the wrong hands any method can be boring. But if you pitch drill at a level that is not so hard as to be impossible and not so easy as to be simplistic, it gives pupils a chance to experience the satisfying feeling of conquering a tricky problem. If it is limited to short and frequent activities, pupils do not get bored. In a major American study of Engelmann's direct instruction method, pupils who were taught using this method outperformed their peers not just on their academic performance, but on affective measures such as self-esteem too.[49] Direct instruction is successful and pupils enjoy succeeding.

We have seen already that a teacher-led and fact-filled approach did not harm Shakespeare's creativity. Now let us look at what frequent practice did for Winston Churchill. Like many of the denizens of our famous public schools, Churchill was not actually that smart. Even compared to other public schoolboys, he was not that smart. He was placed in the bottom set at Harrow School and made to repeat a year three times. He spent a lot of that time doing drills:

> By being so long in the lowest form I gained an immense advantage over the cleverer boys. They all went on to learn Latin and Greek and splendid things like that. But I was taught English. We were considered such dunces that we could learn only English. Mr. Somervell—a most delightful man, to whom my debt is great—was charged with the duty of teaching the stupidest boys the most disregarded thing—namely, to write mere English. He knew how to do it. He taught it as no one else has ever taught it. Not only did we learn English parsing thoroughly, but we also practised continually English analysis. Mr. Somervell had a system of his own. He took a fairly long sentence and broke it up into its components by means of black, red, blue, and green inks. Subject, verb, object: Relative Clauses, Conditional Clauses, Conjunctive and Disjunctive Clauses! Each had its colour and its bracket. It was a kind of drill. We did it almost daily. As I remained in the Third Form three times as long as anyone else, I had three times as much of it. I learned it thoroughly. Thus I got into my bones the essential structure of the ordinary British sentence—which is a noble thing.[50]

That is what drilling can do for you. It turned a boy who was considered a dunce into one of the greatest orators the world has ever known. Compare this with the method Ofsted advocate for teaching Churchill's speeches:

> During one visit, the inspector observed different classes all engaged in identifying and practising skills in persuasive speaking and writing. In the two higher-ability sets, election leaflets were distributed among students working in small groups. Students identified techniques used in the leaflet they were given and then the groups were reformed so that experts in each group were able to talk about similarities and differences and evaluate their relative impact. Finally, the students, working individually, tried their hand at the first section of an election leaflet, taking into account their understanding of points made earlier in the lesson when discussing a speech by Winston Churchill.[51]

The modern understanding we have of how we learn suggests that Churchill's methods are more effective than Ofsted's.

At the end of the previous chapter I considered the possibility that these theorists were not actually hostile to facts, merely to certain methods of teaching them. I think it is fair to conclude here that it is because they are hostile to facts that they are hostile to efficient methods of teaching them. Their hostility to formal fact-learning is not because they think facts are taught better in other ways. It is just a subset of their hostility to facts, and of their misconception of the role of facts in cognition. In the next two chapters, we'll look at some more modern justifications for not teaching facts.

Notes

1   Rousseau, J.-J. *Emile, or Education*. Translated by Barbara Foxley. London: Dent, 1921, 1911, p. 127.
2   Ibid., p. 81.
3   Hickman, L.A. and Alexander, T.M. (eds). *The Essential Dewey. Volume 1, Pragmatism, Education, Democracy*. Bloomington: Indiana University Press, 1998, p. 232.
4   Freire, P. *Pedagogy of the Oppressed*. London: Penguin, 1996, p. 53.
5   Ibid.
6   Archer, D. Philosopher's 'legacy of love'. *Times Educational Supplement* (1997), www.tes.co.uk/article.aspx?storycode=67376 (accessed 3 March 2013).
7   Slater, J. Drill-and-kill spells death to lifelong learning. *Times Educational Supplement* (2005), www.tes.co.uk/article.aspx?storycode=2070945 (accessed 3 March 2013); Ward, H. Rote learning equals maths confusion. *Times Educational Supplement* (2012), www.tes.co.uk/article.aspx?storycode=6263284 (accessed 3 March 2013).
8   Rousseau, J.-J. *Emile, or Education*. Translated by Barbara Foxley. London: Dent, 1921, 1911, p. 77.
9   Freire, P. *Pedagogy of the Oppressed*. London: Penguin, 1996, p. 52.

10 King, A. Making a transition from 'sage on the stage' to 'guide on the side'. *College Teaching* 1993; 41: 30–35.

11 Cunnane, S. To spoon-feed is not to nurture. *Times Higher Education Supplement* (2011), www.timeshighereducation.co.uk/news/to-spoon-feed-is-not-to-nurture/418217.article (accessed 3 March 2013).

12 Ibid.

13 Ibid.

14 Frankel, H. Too tough at the top. *Times Educational Supplement* (2010), www.tes.co.uk/article.aspx?storycode=6034506 (accessed 3 March 2013); Stewart, W. More from the Ofsted school of hard knocks. *Times Educational Supplement* (2012), www.tes.co.uk/article.aspx?storycode=6294044 (accessed 3 March 2013); Britland, M. No notice Ofsted inspections? Bring 'em on! *Guardian* (2012), www.guardian.co.uk/teacher-network/teacher-blog/2012/apr/07/ofsted-inspection-week (accessed 3 March 2013).

15 See, for example: *Times Educational Supplement*. Ebay: great for concert tickets … and Ofsted cheats (2009), www.tes.co.uk/article.aspx?storycode=6029108 (accessed 6 March 2013); Times Educational Supplement Online Resources. Ofsted Guidance (2012), www.tes.co.uk/TaxonomySearchResults.aspx?parametrics=52108,52170,52173&event=23&mode=browse (accessed 6 March 2013); Beere, J. and Gilbert, I. *The Perfect Ofsted Lesson*. Bancyfelin: Crown House Publishing, 2010; Weatheroak Inspections. Helping you make the most of your Ofsted Inspections (2013), www.weatheroakinspections.co.uk/consultancy.htm (accessed 6 March 2013).

16 See this link for the Appendix. http://routledge.com/books/details/9780415746823.

17 These lesson descriptions are taken from the following Ofsted subject reports: Making a mark: art, craft and design education 2008–11, March 2012; Moving English forward: Action to raise standards in English, March 2012; Excellence in English: What we can learn from 12 outstanding schools, May 2011; Geography: Learning to make a world of difference, February 2011; History for all: History in English schools 2007/10, March 2011; Mathematics: Made to measure, May 2012; Modern languages: Achievement and challenge 2007–2010, January 2011; Transforming religious education: Religious education in schools 2006–2009, June 2010; Successful science: An evaluation of science education in England 2007–2010, January 2011.

18 Office for Standards in Education, Children's Services and Skills. Moving English forward: Action to raise standards in English (2012), pp. 52–53, www.ofsted.gov.uk/resources/moving-english-forward (accessed 3 March 2013).

19 Ibid.

20 Office for Standards in Education, Children's Services and Skills. Transforming religious education: Religious education in schools 2006–09 (2010), p. 46, http://dera.ioe.ac.uk/110/1/Transforming%20religious%20education.pdf (accessed 3 March 2013).

21 Office for Standards in Education, Children's Services and Skills. Moving English forward: Action to raise standards in English (2012), p. 45, www.ofsted.gov.uk/resources/moving-english-forward (accessed 3 March 2013).

22 Office for Standards in Education, Children's Services and Skills. Geography: Learning to make a world of difference (2011), p. 43, www.ofsted.gov.uk/resources/geography-learning-make-world-of-difference (accessed 3 March 2013).

23 Office for Standards in Education, Children's Services and Skills. Successful science: An evaluation of science education in England 2007–2010 (2011), pp. 17–18, www.ofsted.gov.uk/resources/successful-science (accessed 3 March 2013).

24 Office for Standards in Education, Children's Services and Skills. Geography: Learning to make a world of difference (2011), p. 46, www.ofsted.gov.uk/resources/geography-learning-make-world-of-difference (accessed 3 March 2013).

25 Office for Standards in Education, Children's Services and Skills. Modern languages: Achievement and challenge 2007–2010 (2011), p. 11, www.ofsted.gov.uk/resources/modern-languages-achievement-and-challenge-2007-2010 (accessed 3 March 2013).

26 Ibid.

27 Office for Standards in Education, Children's Services and Skills. Making a mark: art, craft and design education 2008–11 (2012), p.21, www.ofsted.gov.uk/resources/making-mark-art-craft-and-design-education-2008-11 (accessed 3 March 2013).

28 Ibid.

29 Ibid., p. 8.

30 Office for Standards in Education, Children's Services and Skills. Transforming religious education: Religious education in schools 2006–09 (2010), p. 15, www.ofsted.gov.uk/resources/transforming-religious-education (accessed 6 March 2013).

31 Office for Standards in Education, Children's Services and Skills. Mathematics: Made to measure (2012), p. 26, www.ofsted.gov.uk/resources/mathematics-made-measure (accessed 3 March 2013).

32 Coughlan, S. Ofsted plans to scrap 'satisfactory' label for schools. BBC News (2012), www.bbc.co.uk/news/education-16579644 (accessed 3 March 2013).

33 Office for Standards in Education, Children's Services and Skills. Mathematics: Made to measure (2012), p. 23, www.ofsted.gov.uk/resources/mathematics-made-measure (accessed 3 March 2013).

34 Ibid., p. 24.

35 Ibid., p. 33.

36 Hirsch, E.D. The Knowledge Deficit: Closing the Shocking Education Gap for American Children. Boston: Houghton Mifflin, 2006, pp. 7–8.

37 Bruner, J.S. Some elements of discovery. In: Shulman, L.S. and Keislar, E.R. (eds) Learning by Discovery: A Critical Appraisal. Chicago: Rand McNally, 1966, p. 101.

38 Office for Standards in Education, Children's Services and Skills. Geography: Learning to make a world of difference (2011), p. 43, www.ofsted.gov.uk/resources/geography-learning-make-world-of-difference (accessed 3 March 2013).

39 Ibid.

40 Newton, I. Oxford Dictionary of Quotations. Oxford: Oxford University Press, 2009, p. 574.

41 Ilyich, I. Deschooling Society. London: Marion Boyars, 1971.

42 Office for Standards in Education, Children's Services and Skills. Modern languages: Achievement and challenge 2007–2010 (2011), p. 11, www.ofsted.gov.uk/resources/modern-languages-achievement-and-challenge-2007-2010 (accessed 3 March 2013).

43 Kirschner, P.A., Sweller, J. and Clark, R.E. Why minimal guidance during instruction does not work: An analysis of the failure of constructivist, discovery, problem-based, experiential, and inquiry-based teaching. Educational Psychologist 2006; 41: 75–86.

44 Ibid.

45 Ibid., p. 79.

46 Hattie, J. *Visible Learning: A Synthesis of Over 800 Meta-Analyses Relating to Achievement.* New York: Routledge, 2009, p. 206.

47 Ibid., p. 205.

48 Ibid., p. 204.

49 Adams, G. Project Follow Through: In-depth and beyond. *Effective School Practices* 1996; 15: 43–56.

50 Churchill, W. *A Roving Commission: My Early Life.* New York: C. Scribner's Sons, 1939, p. 16.

51 Office for Standards in Education, Children's Services and Skills. Excellence in English: What we can learn from 12 outstanding schools (2011), pp. 15–16, www. education.gov.uk/publications/eOrderingDownload/100229.pdf (accessed 3 March 2013).

Myth 3

The twenty-first century fundamentally changes everything

Where is the evidence that people believe this and that it has affected education policy and classroom practice?

Theoretical evidence

In the previous two chapters, we saw how influential theory and practice warn against teaching facts. In this chapter and the next, I shall show how false claims about the nature of economic and technological change are used to support the idea that facts are not necessary.

This myth tells us that pupils in the twenty-first century require a completely different education from pupils in previous centuries. Because of changes in technology and changes in the economy, we cannot teach pupils the way we always have done. We saw in the last chapter how factual learning was set up in opposition to conceptual learning, or true understanding. Likewise, in this chapter, I shall show that twenty-first century education is often set up in opposition to nineteenth-century education. Often, one dichotomy is placed on top of the other; twenty-first century skills on one side, nineteenth-century knowledge on the other. Indeed, the phrase 'twenty-first century skills' has become a popular education buzzword, referred to by a range of different people and organisations in and out of education. There is no one central authority determining what these skills are and later on in this chapter I shall give some specific examples from individual institutions; however, the following skills tend to crop up again and again: problem-solving, critical thinking, creativity and interpersonal communication. As far as I know, there is no such thing as twenty-first century knowledge. The rationale for selecting such skills and for suggesting that they are important for our future are twofold.

First, modern technological practices eliminate the need for us to remember and memorise vast quantities of information. We have created memory stores outside our brains – first in books, now in the Internet – which make individual knowledge of every capital of every country in the world, for example, quaint rather than useful. Thus, the nineteenth-century practices of memorising the capital, population and chief products of every country in the world are fairly useless when a second on the Internet can tell you those things. Twenty-first century technological innovation means that our education system needs to stop focusing on facts and start focusing on skills instead. I shall deal more fully with this aspect in the next chapter.

Second, over the last few decades, the economy and the workplace have seen profound changes. New and disruptive technologies have the ability to destroy or decimate entire industries. When entire industries and careers can very quickly become obsolete, traditional bodies of knowledge are no longer of great value. What is the point of having a detailed knowledge of a particular system when that system could be replaced by a better, more efficient one the next day? Indeed, what is the point even of having very specific and detailed skills? In the 1970s, many schools taught secretarial classes, not realising that the rise of the personal computer would very quickly reduce the demand for secretaries. The same is true even in high-tech industries. Polaroid were the world leaders at developing photo negatives quickly. But their technical expertise in this field could not stop the company going bankrupt when demand for chemically developed photographs declined.[1] This is why a lot of the rhetoric of modern education sounds very similar to the rhetoric of modern business consultants. Where educationalists talk of a skills-based curriculum, business schools speak of core competences. Polaroid should have realised that their expertise was not in the detailed and precise knowledge of chemicals and negatives, but in the soaring, overarching skill of producing images quickly. Then, they would not have been blindsided by technological change. Steve Wheeler, the academic and learning technologist, makes these economic concerns clear:

> After all, it is the ability to work in a team, problem solve on the fly, and apply creative solutions that will be the common currency in the world of future work. Being able to think critically and create a professional network will be the core competencies of the 21st Century knowledge worker ... You see, the world of work is in constant change, and that change is accelerating.
>
> My 16 year old son has just embarked on training to become a games designer. If, when I was his age I had told my careers teacher that I wanted to be a games designer, he would have asked me whether I wanted to make cricket bats or footballs. Jobs are appearing that didn't exist even a year or two ago. Other jobs that people expected to be in for life are disappearing or gone forever. Ask the gas mantel fitters or VHS repair technicians. Ask the tin miners, the lamplighters or the typewriter repair people. Er, sorry you can't ask them. They don't exist anymore.[2]

In 2003, the government released a white paper which made these links between actual economic change and the necessity for educational change. It was a joint publication of the Department for Education and Skills (now the Department of Education), the Department for Trade and Industry (now the Department for Business, Innovation & Skills), Her Majesty's Treasury and the Department for Work and Pensions and it was called *21st Century Skills: Realising Our Potential: Individuals, Employers, Nation.* That is how important skills are – at the heart not just of education but of a successful country and economy. It argued that 'the global economy has made largely extinct the notion of a "job for life". The imperative now is employability for life … that is dependent on raising our skills game'.[3] The response of the government to this changing economic world was to establish a number of organisations and programmes dedicated to improving the nation's skills: the Learning and Skills Council, the National Skills Strategy, Skills for Life, the Skills Alliance.

At around about the same time, educationalists were expanding on this issue. In a 1999 report, the National Advisory Committee on Creative and Cultural Education (NACCCE) said that:

> We live in a fast moving world. While employers continue to demand high academic standards, they also now want more. They want people who can adapt, see connections, innovate, communicate and work with others … Many businesses are paying for courses to promote creative abilities, to teach the skills and attitudes that are now essential for economic success but which our education system is not designed to promote.[4]

It also made it clear that our current system is not fit for the twenty-first century:

> The foundations of the present education system were laid at the end of the nineteenth century. They were designed to meet the needs of a world that was being transformed by industrialisation. We are publishing this report at the dawn of a new century. The challenges we face now are of the same magnitude, but they are of a different character. The task is not to do better now what we set out to do then: it is to rethink the purposes, methods and scale of education in our new circumstances.[5]

So, the lessons of the modern economy and the twenty-first century seem to be that an education that requires you to learn specific stuff will doom you to obsolescence and irrelevance. Instead, education should focus on the acquisition of skills, preferably transferable skills, which will allow the individual to adapt quickly to the inevitable change that the twenty-first century will bring.

The most successful intellectual ideas are those that go beyond the circles of a few intellectuals or policy wonks and instead achieve some kind of mainstream currency. We saw in the previous chapter the way that Dickens's creation of Thomas Gradgrind is used in popular discussions about education and fact-learning. The idea of twenty-first century skills has also achieved a more mainstream popularity. Sir Ken Robinson, who chaired the NACCCE, has gained a huge audience through his popular online videos about his views on twenty-first century skills. *Changing Education Paradigms*, which is part of the Royal Society of Arts's (RSA) Animate series, has been viewed by over nine million people.[6] It poses the question: 'How do we educate our children to take their place in the economies of the 21st century, given that we can't anticipate what the economy will look like at the end of next week?' His answer, in short, is that we need to move our education system towards a model based more on collaboration and creativity. His Technology, Entertainment, Design (TED) talk, *Do Schools Kill Creativity?*, has been viewed by over four million people. It starts by reminding us that pupils who are at school now will retire in 2065.[7] How can we know what these pupils will need to know in 2065 when we do not even know what the world will be like in five years?

Another good example of how these ideas have reached the mainstream is the YouTube video 'Shift Happens'. This video was made by an American high school teacher and has since been viewed on YouTube over five million times.[8] On my teacher training course, the entire cohort of nearly 300 trainees were shown the video on a big screen in the lecture hall, after which a lecturer gave a speech that accepted most of its assertions. This video highlights some startling facts about demographic and technological change and uses them to make some even more startling conclusions. Among its frightening claims are the following: that the pupils we teach today will be doing jobs that do not exist yet, and that because of the rapid rate of technological change, by the time a student got to the final year of a degree course, what they learned in their first year would be outdated. The implication was clear: there was no point in wasting time teaching them knowledge that would be useless to their future careers.

These ideas clearly owe a lot to modern economic theorists and management consultants. It is perhaps surprising, therefore, that the UK teaching unions, who are generally quite sceptical about modern theories of the economy, have been so keen to embrace these ideas. But embrace them they have. Russell Hobby, General Secretary of the National Association of Head Teachers, supports the skills-based curriculum in precisely these terms. In a blog, he argued that 'demand in the workplace for "routine cognitive skills" – based on easily digestible knowledge (like lists of kings and queens) – is in decline, as these tasks are automated and outsourced … the future lies in problem solving and interpersonal skills'.[9] In 2006, the Association of Teachers and Lecturers published a position statement, titled *Subject to Change*, which stated that: 'A twenty-first century curriculum cannot have the transfer of knowledge at its core for the simple reason that the selection of what is required has become problematic in an information rich age.'[10] It drew on research from the Organisation for Economic Co-operation and Development, which looked at different types of knowledge and predicted the following:

As access to information becomes easier and less expensive, the skills and competencies relating to the selection and efficient use of information become more crucial … Capabilities for selecting relevant and disregarding irrelevant information, recognising patterns in information, interpreting and decoding information as well as learning new and forgetting old skills are in increasing demand.[11]

The idea is that if we teach pupils bodies of knowledge, we will doom them to a life seeking out ever-diminishing manual jobs for ever-diminishing pay while their skills-educated peers, unburdened by knowledge, could whizz around the country problem-solving and interpersonalising in return for vast sums of money.

Modern practice

These ideas have influenced a number of approaches to classroom teaching. Perhaps the most significant approach is that taken by the RSA, the famous and historic multidisciplinary organisation. They have developed a new secondary curriculum called Opening Minds which is designed to meet this twenty-first century challenge. Its rationale is as follows:

> What and how children should be taught is a question which should be explored as both society and technology change and develop. With this in mind the RSA set out to explore how teaching and learning could better equip young people to meet the challenges of the 21st century.[12]

They concluded that there were five essential skills needed for the twenty-first century. These skills, rather than subject disciplines, are the organising principles of the Opening Minds curriculum, which is used by about 200 English schools (approximately 6 per cent of secondary schools in England).[13] The five skills, or competences, are as follows: citizenship; learning; managing information; relating to people; and managing situations.[14] The RSA Opening Minds programme is designed so that 'children plan their work, organise their own time and explore their own ways of learning'.[15] In the flagship schools that have adopted this curriculum, most of the curriculum time is organised around projects, not subjects. For example, at Cardinal Heenan Catholic High School, 19 out of the 25 lessons a week in year 7 are given over to the following six half-termly projects: I am What I am; Time Travelling with the Doctor; In my Liverpool Home; Pressgang; Going Global; and Flaming Challenge.[16] Cardinal Heenan is one of seven schools which 'have been awarded RSA Opening Minds Training School status. These are schools that have been assessed as being "good" or "outstanding" by Ofsted and, following a rigorous application and assessment process have been designated as leading practitioners of Opening Minds'.[17]

At least one of the new English free schools has used the ideas of twenty-first century skills to organise their curriculum. Peter Hyman, head of a free school in Newham, has gone so far as to name his school School 21, because it is organised around twenty-first century skills. For him, there are six important concepts: professionalism, eloquence, grit, spark, craftsmanship and expertise.[18]

A 2009 Ofsted report into English encouraged schools to change their approach to the subject to meet the challenges of the twenty-first century:

> Teachers need to decide what English should look like as a subject in the 21st century and how they can improve the motivation and achievement of pupils who traditionally do less well in the subject. To engage them more successfully, schools need to provide a more dynamic and productive curriculum in English that reflects the changing nature of society and pupils' literacy needs.[19]

In practice, that meant adopting approaches that 'motivated students, helped them to develop their skills in real contexts, provided a clear reason and audience for their work, and made learning relevant'.[20] An example of such an approach is this primary school lesson:

> The teachers ensured that the pupils had experiences to help them formulate ideas and give a context to and content for their writing. For example, Year 3/4 pupils spent an hour on the school field, trying out hoeing, digging and bird-scaring before recounting the life of a Victorian child as a farm labourer. The teachers said that such activities helped the pupils to empathise and provide detail in their writing.[21]

For one final example of how twenty-first century skills might practically work in schools, consider the recommendations of Martin Johnson, author of the Association of Teachers and Lecturers' (ATL) report into the curriculum. He argued that the school curriculum should prioritise life skills such as walking rather than 'totalitarian' knowledge:

> There's a lot to learn about how to walk. If you were going out for a Sunday afternoon stroll you might walk one way. If you're trying to catch a train you might walk in another way and if you are doing a cliff walk you might walk in another way. If you are carrying a pack, there's a technique in that. We need a nation of people who understand their bodies and can use their bodies effectively.[22]

Why is this a myth?

It is of course true that the skills often defined as being twenty-first century are very important. Problem-solving, creative thinking, critical thinking and relating to people are all incredibly important skills. There is not one skill listed above that I would cavil at. But there is nothing uniquely twenty-first century about them. Mycenaean Greek craftsmen had to work with others, adapt and innovate. It is quite patronising to suggest that no one before the year 2000 ever needed to think critically, solve problems, communicate, collaborate, create, innovate or read. Human beings have been doing most of these things for quite a long time. The alphabet, a relatively late development of civilisation, was invented in the twenty-first century BC.[23] It probably is true that in the future, more and more people will need these skills, and that there will be fewer economic opportunities for people who do not have these skills. But that would suggest to me that we need to make sure that everyone gets the education that was in the past reserved for the elite. That is not redefining education for the twenty-first century; it is giving everyone the chance to get a traditional education.

And that is where the real problem with the concept of twenty-first century education lies. To the extent that it says that creativity and problem-solving are important, it is merely banal; to the extent that it says such skills are unique to the twenty-first century, it is false but harmless; to the extent that it proposes certain ways of achieving these aims, it is actually pernicious. This is because, very often, the movement for twenty-first century skills is a codeword for removing knowledge from the curriculum, and removing knowledge from the curriculum will ensure that pupils do not develop twenty-first century skills.

Of course, one way the twenty-first century really is different from other eras is in the incredible power of technology. But this difference, while real, tends to lead on to two more education fallacies. First, it tells us that advances in technology remove the need for pupils to memorise anything: that is, you can always just Google it. I show why this is false in Chapter 4. Second, it is used to support the idea that traditional bodies of knowledge are outmoded. There is just so much knowledge nowadays, and it is changing all the time, so there is no point learning any of it to begin with. We saw the ATL argue, for example, that: 'A twenty-first century curriculum cannot have the transfer of knowledge at its core for the simple reason that the selection of what is required has become problematic in an information rich age.'[24] The video Shift Happens tells us that 1.5 exabytes of unique new information are generated each year, and that the amount of new technical information is doubling each year. It then concludes that this flow of new information means that for students starting a four-year college or technical degree, half of what they learn in their first year will be outdated by their third year of study.[25] This is simply not true. Of course people make new discoveries all the time, but a lot of those new discoveries do not disprove or supersede previous ones; in fact, they are more likely to build on previous discoveries and require intimate knowledge of them. The fundamental foundations of most disciplines are rarely, if ever, completely disproved. The extent to which scientific revolutions really overturn the fundamentals is often exaggerated. Ben Goldacre puts it thus:

> One of the key humanities graduates' parodies of science [is that] science is temporary, changeable, constantly revising itself, like a transient fad. Scientific findings, the argument goes, are therefore dismissible.

While this is true at the bleeding edges of various research fields, it's worth bearing in mind that Archimedes has been right about why things float for a couple of millennia. He also understood why levers work, and Newtonian physics will probably be right about the behaviour of snooker balls forever.[26]

When it comes to mathematics, there is even less chance of revision. In a foreword to Carl Boyer's *A History of Mathematics*, Isaac Asimov argued the following:

> Only in mathematics is there no significant correction – only extension. Once the Greeks had developed the deductive method, they were correct in what they did, correct for all time. Euclid was incomplete and his work has been extended enormously, but it has not had to be corrected. His theorems are, every one of them, valid to this day.[27]

Universities can turn out as many exabytes of information as they like; they are unlikely to disprove Pythagoras's theorem or improve on Euripides's tragedies. And there are very many such ancient and fundamental ideas and inventions that have stood the test of time: perhaps more than we are willing to admit. The alphabet and the numbering system, for example, are two of the most valuable inventions we have. Respectively, the origins of these inventions are in approximately 2000 BC and 3000 BC.[28] They have been refined and enhanced through the ages, but their basic principles show no signs of wearing out or being superseded. All of the most modern and advanced technological devices depend on them in one way or another. Indeed, if anything, the sheer proliferation of knowledge should lead to selective bodies of knowledge becoming *more* important, as mechanisms for separating the wheat from the vast amounts of chaff.

The scientific and technological innovators who make the headlines tend to be quite young. But behind the headlines, the median age for the first scientific discovery has been increasing steadily over the decades.[29] That is because to make a scientific breakthrough, first of all you have to reach the frontiers of knowledge in your discipline. As scientific knowledge has advanced over the decades, that frontier has got further and further away, which means that it takes researchers more and more time to reach it. What this should show us is that making a new scientific discovery requires an intimate understanding of what has gone before. In Newton's famous words, scientific giants are standing on the shoulders of others. Indeed, we all benefit from the painfully accumulated knowledge of the generations that have gone before us. One of the wonders of being alive today is that a person of average intelligence is able to know things that some of the greatest minds of centuries past were ignorant of. Perhaps the most fascinating aspect of the study of ancient history is to see the struggles of humans who were no more or less innately intelligent than we are, but who did not have the benefit, as we do, of thousands of years of accumulated knowledge. The historian John Roberts has this to say:

> The rapidity with which humanity has achieved so much since prehistoric times can be accounted for quite simply: there are many more of us upon whose talents humanity can draw and, more important still, human achievements are essentially cumulative. They rest upon a heritage itself accumulating at, as it were, compound interest. Primitive societies had far less inherited advantage in the bank. This makes the magnitude of their greatest steps forward all the more amazing.[30]

He also goes so far as to say that civilisation is the result of 'the accumulation of a capital of experience and knowledge'.[31]

The irony, of course, is that if the idea that in the twenty-first century we should be sceptical about teaching our pupils content has any validity, it is actually that the newer the idea, the more likely it is to become obsolete. If something has proved itself valuable over 5,000 years, it is a good bet that it will be useful for the next 100; if something has only been valuable for the last 50 or 20, then we cannot be nearly so certain. Microfiche readers and MiniDisc players have more chance of becoming obsolete than the alphabet and the numerical system. Specific industry and job-related knowledge and skills do change and become outdated over short periods of time; the fundamental knowledge and skills that underpin them do not, and these are what we should teach in school. Larry Sanger, the co-founder of Wikipedia and clearly a man who does not lack for technological understanding, makes this point brilliantly:

> The specific skills for the work world were, and largely still are, learned on the job. So let's see, which would have been better for me to learn back in 1985, when I was 17: all the ins and outs of WordPerfect and BASIC, or U.S. History? There should be no question at all: what I learned about history will remain more or less the same, subject to a few corrections; skills in WordPerfect and BASIC are not longer needed.[32]

So the newer the idea, the more sceptical we should be about teaching it in school, and the older the idea, the more likely it has stood the test of time. Yet of course, the twenty-first century skills movement draws exactly the opposite conclusion. Its mantra is about being constantly new, constantly up to date, always on the cutting edge. But nothing dates so fast as the cutting edge.

The guilty secret of the twenty-first century skills advocates is that it is *their* ideas which are rather old hat and outdated. Diane Ravitch notes how, at the beginning of the twentieth century, many educators wanted to throw away traditional knowledge and embrace twentieth century skills.[33] There is little difference between what Martin Johnson calls a twenty-first century approach to teaching and what John Dewey was advocating at the dawn of the twentieth.

There is very little difference between the types of projects the RSA are advocating and the types that proliferated at various points in the United States and the UK from the late nineteenth century onwards.[34] Such projects have consistently failed in a variety of different settings, for reasons I shall examine more fully in Chapter 6. All over the world, successful education systems use subject disciplines to organise their curriculum, not abstract skills.[35]

The most depressing thing about all of this, therefore, is that old ideas that are thoroughly discredited are being warmed over and presented as being at the cutting edge. And it is particularly ironic that, as we will see in the next chapter, the actual cutting-edge science is telling us to do the complete opposite of what most of the twenty-first century skills advocates want.

Notes

1   Christensen, C.M., Horn, M.B. and Johnson, C.W. *Disrupting Class: How Disruptive Innovation Will Change the Way the World Learns*. New York: McGraw-Hill, 2008, p. 97.
2   Wheeler, S. Content as curriculum? (2011), http://steve-wheeler.blogspot. co.uk/2011/12/content-as-curriculum.html (accessed 3 March 2013). As a side note, it is worth pointing out here that tin miners most certainly still do exist. Tin mining employs thousands of people in China and Indonesia and much modern technology could not exist without tin; it 'is so crucial to electronics that tin is the most common metal used by Apple suppliers, according to data Apple made public earlier this year'. From Simpson, C. The deadly tin inside your smartphone (2012), www.businessweek.com/articles/2012-08-23/the-deadly-tin-inside-your-ipad#p1 (accessed 6 March 2013).
3   Department for Education and Skills. *21st Century Skills: Realising Our Potential: Individuals, Employers, Nation*. Norwich: HMSO, 2003, p. 11.
4   National Advisory Committee on Creative and Cultural Education. All our futures: Creativity, culture and education (1999), p. 14, http://sirkenrobinson.com/skr/ pdf/allourfutures.pdf (accessed 4 March 2013).
5   Ibid., p. 16.
6   Robinson, K. Changing education paradigms (2012), www.youtube.com/ watch?v=zDZFcDGpL4U (accessed 4 March 2013).
7   TED. Ken Robinson says schools kill creativity (2006), www.ted.com/talks/ken_ robinson_says_schools_kill_creativity.html (accessed 4 March 2013).
8   Fisch, K. and McLeod, S. Shift happens (2007), www.youtube.com/watch?v=ljbI-363A2Q (accessed 3 March 2013).
9   Hobby, R. Russell Hobby stops biting his tongue with the CBI (2010), www.naht. org.uk/welcome/news-and-media/blogs/russell-hobby-general-secretary/?blogpost=362 (accessed 3 March 2013).
10 Association of Teachers and Lecturers. Subject to change: New thinking on the curriculum (2007), www.atl.org.uk/Images/Subject%20to%20change.pdf (accessed 4 March 2013).

11 Organisation for Economic Co-operation and Development. The knowledge-based economy (1996), p. 13, www.cercetareservicii.ase.ro/resurse/Documente/THE%20KNOWLEDGE-BASED%20ECONOMY.pdf (accessed 4 March 2013).

12 Royal Society of Arts' Opening Minds. Why was RSA Opening Minds developed? (2013), www.rsaopeningminds.org.uk/about-rsa-openingminds/why-was-opening-minds-developed/ (accessed 4 March 2013).

13 Royal Society of Arts Opening Minds. What is RSA Opening Minds? (2013), www.rsaopeningminds.org.uk/about-rsa-openingminds/ (accessed 4 March 2013); in 2010, there were 3,332 maintained secondary schools, city technology colleges and academies in England. Department for Education. Statistical first release: Schools, pupils, and their characteristics, January 2010 (provisional), Table 2a (2010), www.education.gov.uk/rsgateway/DB/SFR/s000925/sfr09-2010.pdf (accessed 6 March 2013).

14 Royal Society of Arts Opening Minds. What is RSA Opening Minds? (2013), www.rsaopeningminds.org.uk/about-rsa-openingminds/ (accessed 4 March 2013).

15 Royal Society of Arts Opening Minds. RSA Opening Minds competence framework (2013), www.rsaopeningminds.org.uk/about-rsa-openingminds/competences/ (accessed 4 March 2013).

16 Cardinal Heenan Catholic High School. The curriculum: Key Stage 3 (2012), www.cardinal-heenan.org.uk/index.php?option=com_content&view=article&id=77&Itemid=87&lang=en (accessed 4 March 2013).

17 Royal Society of Arts Opening Minds. RSA Opening Minds Training School network (2013), www.rsaopeningminds.org.uk/accreditation-of-opening-minds/training-school-network/ (accessed 4 March 2013).

18 New Statesman. What we should teach children (2012), www.newstatesman.com/politics/politics/2012/07/what-we-should-teach-children (accessed 4 March 2013).

19 Office for Standards in Education, Children's Services and Skills. English at the crossroads: an evaluation of English in primary and secondary schools 2005/08 (2009), p. 54, www.ofsted.gov.uk/resources/english-crossroads-evaluation-of-english-primary-and-secondary-schools-200508 (accessed 4 March 2013).

20 Ibid., p. 22.

21 Ibid., p. 26.

22 *Guardian.* Teachers' union calls for lessons in walking (2007), www.guardian.co.uk/education/2007/mar/30/schools.uk (accessed 4 March 2013).

23 Sacks, D. *Language Visible: Unravelling the Mystery of the Alphabet From A-Z.* Toronto: Alfred A Knopf, 2003, pp. xiv, 37.

24 Association of Teachers and Lecturers. *Subject to change: New thinking on the curriculum* (2006), www.atl.org.uk/Images/Subject%20to%20change%20-%20curriculum%20PS%202006.pdf (accessed 6 March 2013).

25 Fisch, K. and McLeod, S. Shift happens (2007), www.youtube.com/watch?v=ljbI-363A2Q (accessed 3 March 2013).

26 Goldacre, B. *Bad Science.* London: Harper Perennial, 2009, p. 237.

27 Asimov, I. Foreword to the second edition. In: Merzbach, U.C. and Boyer, C. *A History of Mathematics.* 3rd edn. Hoboken: John Wiley & Sons, 2011, p. xi.

28 Sacks, D. *Language Visible: Unravelling the Mystery of the Alphabet From A-Z.* Toronto: Alfred A Knopf, 2003, pp. xiv, 37; Merzbach, U.C. and Boyer, C. *A History of Mathematics.* 3rd edn. Hoboken: John Wiley & Sons, 2011, p. 10.

29 Jones, B.F. and National Bureau of Economic Research. Age and great invention. *Review of Economics and Statistics* 2010; 92: 1–14; Jones, B.F. The burden of knowledge and the death of the Renaissance man: Is innovation getting harder? *Review of Economic Studies* 2009, 76: 283–317.

30 Roberts, J.M. *Ancient History: From the First Civilisations to the Renaissance*, London: Duncan Baird, 2004, p. 64.

31 Ibid., p. 11.

32 Sanger, L. An example of educational anti-intellectualism (2011), http://larrysanger. org/2011/12/an-example-of-educational-anti-intellectualism/ (accessed 4 March 2013).

33 Ravitch, D. 21st century skills: An old familiar song (2013), http://commoncore. org/_docs/diane.pdf (accessed 4 March 2013).

34 Ravitch, D. *Left Back: A Century of Battles over School Reform*. New York: Touchstone, 2000.

35 Common Core Foundation. Why we're behind: What top nations teach their students but we don't (2009), www.commoncore.org/_docs/CCreport_ whybehind.pdf (accessed 4 March 2013); Ruddock, G. and Sainsbury, M. Comparison of the core primary curriculum in England to those of other high performing countries (2008), www.education.gov.uk/publications/eOrdering Download/DCSF-RW048v2.pdf (accessed 6 March 2013).

Myth 4

You can always just look it up

Where is the evidence that people believe this and that it has affected education policy and classroom practice?

Theoretical evidence

We saw in the previous chapter that the changing economy and technology of the twenty-first century often provide a rationale for the teaching of twenty-first century skills. The central plank of this argument is that the existence of new information technologies means we do not have to worry as much about teaching facts. This argument did not begin with the invention of Google. A famous phrasing of this theory is frequently attributed to Albert Einstein: 'You don't have to know everything, you just have to know where to find it.' The website Quote Investigator (http://quoteinvestigator.com/) shows that while this quotation is frequently attributed to Einstein, he did not in fact say it. However, at the beginning of the twentieth century many people did express similar sentiments. The following sayings appeared in American periodicals in 1914 and 1917, respectively:

> Educated people are not those who know everything, but rather those who know where to find, at a moment's notice, the information they desire.

> Someone has said that the cleverest people are not those who know everything, but those who know where to look for and find any information that is at the moment required.[1]

Libraries, filing systems and books of clippings were where you needed to go to find information then. With the invention of the Internet and search engines, accessing information has become phenomenally easier, and arguments for the unimportance of actually knowing things yourself have become progressively bolder. For example, here is Steve Wheeler, education professor at the University of Plymouth:

Occasionally I hear someone saying 'I'm glad I took Latin at school', and then arguing that it helped them to discover the name of a fish they caught whilst out angling on holiday. Well, knowing that *thalassoma bifasciatum* is a blue-headed wrasse may be wonderful for one's self esteem. It may impress your friends during a pub quiz, but it won't get you a job … and was it really worth all those hours learning how to conjugate amo, amas, amat simply to be able to one day identify a strange fish, when all you need to do in the digital mobile age is Google it?

The question is, how much do children now need to learn in school that is knowledge based? Do children really need to know what a phrasal verb is, or that William Shakespeare died in 1616 when what they really need to be able to do is write a coherent and convincing job application or construct a relevant CV? We call this type of learning *declarative* knowledge, because it is 'knowing that' – in other words, the learning of facts … Knowing how – or *procedural knowledge* – will be a greater asset for most young people.[2]

In all these arguments, procedural knowledge, or knowing how, is both separated from and privileged above declarative knowledge, or knowing what. It is a rephrasing of the same dichotomy between knowledge and skills that we have seen already in previous chapters. It is also an idea that has great currency. In 2008, Don Tapscott, the influential Canadian businessman and writer, made the following case:

> Teachers are no longer the fountain of knowledge; the internet is. Kids should learn about history to understand the world and why things are the way they are. But they don't need to know all the dates. It is enough that they know about the Battle of Hastings, without having to memorise that it was in 1066. They can look that up and position it in history with a click on Google.[3]

His ideas have found some support among teachers in England. In 2012, the Association of Teachers and Lecturers teaching union debated the curriculum at their annual conference. One of the speakers, Jon Overton, set the delegates a simple task:

> [He] asked delegates to find Mozart's birth date using their smartphones. The answer – 27 January, 1756 – was shouted from the floor in seconds.
> We are no longer in an age where a substantial 'fact bank' in our heads is required, he said. We need to equip our young people with skills; interpersonal skills, enquiry skills, the ability to innovate.[4]

In 2011, Paul Fisher, head of a primary school in Stafford, commented: 'Why teach them about the Battle of Hastings when they have got Google? For us, it is about teaching them how to learn.'[5]

The theory is that technology can liberate us from the burden of having to know things.

Modern practice

This myth leads to two claims about classroom practice. First, you do not need to worry about teaching too much knowledge or memorising facts, because pupils will be able to look up all the knowledge they need. Second, you should teach research skills and practise researching information because that will enable pupils to access these vast knowledge databases.

Practically, this means that instead of spending time teaching facts, you spend time teaching pupils all-purpose research and investigation skills. It is for this reason that managing information is one of the RSA Opening Minds curriculum's core competences. Managing information is subdivided into two categories:

> *Research* – students develop a range of techniques for accessing, evaluating and differentiating information and have learned how to analyse, synthesise and apply it.
> *Reflection* – students understand the importance of reflecting and applying critical judgement and learn how to do so.[6]

Instead of the teacher transmitting information, the students develop 'techniques for accessing, evaluating and differentiating information'.[7] Futurelab, a UK educational charity, promotes a similar approach to the curriculum:

> The ability to interpret and question sources of information has arguably become increasingly important in a world in which the internet is the dominant research tool. The problem is that, as digital media have proliferated and extended into many areas of public and private life, it has become increasingly difficult to decode the content, purpose and possible outcomes of what is communicated via media. This is a challenge of legibility. Do people have the ability to read the communications produced in a variety of new media where it is not clear what constitutes authority and trustworthiness?[8]

For Futurelab, the challenge is for schools to develop their pupils' critical thinking skills by 'class discussion about sources of information and differing opinions ... along with the development of questioning skills'.[9]

We saw in Chapter 2 that Ofsted are not keen on lessons which involve the teacher imparting information by talking, for example. But they have less of a problem with lessons where pupils are learning information by researching it on the Internet, or indeed by researching it through other means. The following history lesson was praised as one which displayed 'the most effective subject pedagogy':

Students in Year 9 were given the task of investigating changes in bombing strategy, comparing the First and Second World Wars. They devised their enquiries and structured them appropriately with individual guidance from the class teacher. Each student had her or his own laptop and used both academic and general interest websites to research data and find different interpretations. This valuable exercise led to some valid independent work. It was enhanced by the fact that, although students were given a broad framework and a key question which they were required to answer, the structure of the enquiry was not prescribed and the students were able to develop their own styles and structures.[10]

This geography lesson involved seven-year-olds using the Internet to do research:

Year 2 pupils were working on Fizzbooks to research what they could find out from the internet about Tocuaro (a Mexican village). They had been introduced to this new technology the day before and could use it with ease and explain what it was and how you used it. They made good use of the stylus to zoom in on pictorial images. Pupils worked in pairs to produce their own notes of their findings.[11]

Similarly, this art lesson involved minimal teacher transmission of knowledge about a completely new topic:

Students in Year 9 worked in teams of four, each team given the name of a contemporary artist, craftmaker or designer. They were set the challenge of finding out about their creative practitioner, and who or what had influenced their work. The teacher's grouping together of students with different interests and strengths paid dividends. For example one group deployed a student skilled in the use of digital media to present their findings graphically, and a different student who enjoyed experimenting made samples showing how technique had been refined. A particularly confident speaker in the group researched background information to use.[12]

In this example, Ofsted compare two lessons within a school. One lesson was part of a new, innovative curriculum, and one was part of the older curriculum:

Staff who were unfamiliar with the new developments did not always capitalise on the pupils' improved learning skills, with the result that the pupils sometimes felt uncomfortable when they returned to what they described as the 'old type' of lessons. In one school, for example, the pupils had become used to ready access to their wireless laptops as part of a research-based approach to learning. This encouraged them to work independently and think more widely about aspects of their work. In lessons that did not use the same approach and relied heavily on exposition from the teacher, the pupils became restless and their concentration faltered. This highlighted the importance of ensuring that all staff understand the benefits of new approaches and are able to meet pupils' higher expectations.[13]

Ofsted have never explicitly said that pupils no longer need to memorise facts because you can research them on the Internet. However, in practice, their advice and examples suggest something similar. Their subject reports rarely praise teachers teaching facts and pupils memorising them, but they do encourage lessons where pupils research information on the Internet. There is a clear assumption that you can rely on the knowledge being out there.

Why is this a myth?

As with many of these myths, this one contains part of a real truth. Information technologies are incredible and transformative. The type of research that even 15 years ago would have taken days of trawling through physical archives can now be accomplished in a fraction of the time. The Internet has also opened up access to knowledge. When important knowledge such as newspaper archives, for example, was stored in a physical archive, the numbers of people who could access it were limited. Now that many important archives of knowledge are online, people from around the world can access these archives without having to pay for travel or take time off work. Anyone who cares about education has to celebrate these technological breakthroughs, all the good they have already done, and all the potential they have to do good in the future.

However, as we have seen, many people go beyond that. Some educationalists make the specific claim that such technologies render memory and the teaching of facts less important; in practice, this means that the limited time that is given over to the transmission of facts is very largely given over not to the teacher transmitting facts, but the pupil looking them up using new technologies.

Essentially, this specific claim is a myth because of the evidence presented in Chapter 1. I shall briefly recap here. Long-term memory is not a bolted on part of the brain's architecture. It is instead integral to all our mental processes. When we try to solve any problem, we draw on all the knowledge that we have committed to long-term memory. The more knowledge we have, the more types of problems we are able to solve. The reason why we need that knowledge in long-term memory and cannot rely on it being in the environment is that our working memories are limited. Working memory can only hold three to seven new pieces of information at once.

It is for this reason that modern technology cannot do the memorising for us. We cannot rely on just looking it up, and we cannot outsource memory to

Google. This is because we need those facts in our long-term memory to free up space in our working memory. Looking something up on Google uses up that space in our working memory and means we do not have that space available to process the new information or to combine it with other information. This is why it is so important for young pupils to learn number bonds and the times tables.

If you try to do the multiplication 14 × 7 and you know your times tables very well, then effectively all you have to do is recall 10 × 7 from long-term memory and 4 × 7 and add them together. If you have not memorised your times tables, then you will have to work out each sum individually, and the likelihood is that, by the time you have worked out the first part of the sum, you will have forgotten the second part. This phenomenon – forgetting the second part of the question because you are so busy working out the first part – is one that children and indeed adults frequently run up against, and it is a problem of the limitation of working memory. By memorising frequently used bits of information like number bonds and the times tables, we ensure that pupils can solve more complex problems without overloading their working memory.

It is for these reasons that it is worthwhile memorising things even if we understand the conceptual process used to get them. That is, even if a child conceptually understands how the times tables work, it is still worthwhile for the child to memorise them. It is the same reason why it is important to know the correct spelling even if you know how to look words up in a dictionary. Knowledge that is used frequently and that is at the basis of so many other problems and tasks needs to be known really, really well. We need to be able to recall it automatically and instantly, without strain.

The other important reason why you cannot just look it up is that looking it up actually presupposes an awful lot of knowledge. Imagine the typical dictionary entry for a word you do not know. It is often itself full of complex words and knowledge. Someone who already possesses a great deal of knowledge in their long-term memory will be able to make sense of the definition. However, someone who does not have this background knowledge will not be able to do so. This background knowledge is the schema that helps you make sense of new knowledge.

This is why when we ask pupils to look things up in a dictionary or thesaurus we do not always get the intended results. The scientist George Miller used exactly this process to show why background knowledge matters. He asked a group of pupils to use a dictionary to learn new words. Their lack of knowledge about the words they were looking up rendered the process useless, if quite humorous. Some of the sentences they came up with will be familiar to anyone who has done a similar activity with pupils:

'Mrs. Morrow stimulated the soup.' (That is she stirred it up.)
'Our family erodes a lot.' (That is they eat out.)
'Me and my parents correlate, because without them I wouldn't be here.'

'I was meticulous about falling off the cliff.'
'I relegated my pen pal's letter to her house.'[14]

I can recall asking a pupil to use a thesaurus to improve his vocabulary and getting back the sentence: 'I am congenial at football.'

The same is true of looking things up on the Internet. Unless we already know a reasonable amount about the topic being discussed, reference sources will be of limited value. E.D. Hirsch has this to say:

> There is a consensus in cognitive psychology that it takes knowledge to gain knowledge. Those who repudiate a fact-filled curriculum on the grounds that kids can always look things up miss the paradox that de-emphasising factual knowledge actually disables children from looking things up effectively. To stress process at the expense of factual knowledge actually hinders children from learning to learn. Yes, the Internet has placed a wealth of information at our fingertips. But to be able to use that information—to absorb it, to add to our knowledge—we must already possess a storehouse of knowledge. That is the paradox disclosed by cognitive research.[15]

It is for this reason that encouraging pupils to go off on their own and research things is often a very ineffective strategy. Futurelab, the organisation I cited previously, do at least recognise one of the very common pitfalls with asking pupils to research a topic on the Internet:

> Teachers commonly report students 'copying and pasting' swathes of often only vaguely relevant, sometimes incorrect, information into a document and thinking they have 'done research' without ever engaging with meaning.[16]

This was precisely my experience of setting research tasks. But the reason why pupils do this is not because they are trying to annoy us, but because they do not have enough knowledge to be able to engage with meaning and work out what is and is not relevant and correct. When you read a new text, it is estimated that you need to know the meaning of 95 per cent of the vocabulary in the text to understand it.[17] If you do not, then understanding breaks down and it is very easy for conceptual errors to take hold. And a great deal of the texts we encounter in reference guides and on the Internet have very complex vocabulary. Take this example Hirsch gives of a dictionary definition of 'planet':

> Imagine an expert and a novice looking up the entry 'planets' on the Internet and finding the following:
> planet—any of the non-luminous bodies that revolve around the sun. The term 'planet' is sometimes used to include the asteroids, but

excludes the other members of the solar system, comets, and meteoroids. By extension, any similar body discovered revolving around another star would be called a planet.

A well-informed person would learn a good deal from this entry, if, for example, he was uncertain about whether asteroids, comets, and meteoroids should be called planets. A novice, even one who 'thinks scientifically,' would learn less. Since he wouldn't know what planets are, he probably wouldn't know what asteroids, comets, and meteoroids are. Even the simple phrase 'revolving around another star' would be mystifying, because he probably wouldn't know that the sun is a star. Equally puzzling would be the phrase 'other members of the solar system,' since the term 'solar system' already requires knowing what a planet is. An imaginative novice would no doubt make some fortunate guesses after a rather long time. But, looking things up turns out to have an element of Catch 22; you already need to know something about the subject to look it up effectively.[18]

I once asked a class of pupils to use the Internet to research the life of Charles Dickens and prepare a small presentation on it. One pupil managed to confuse the life of Dickens with that of one of his characters, Pip from *Great Expectations*. I am not quite sure how he managed this, but I suspect that at the heart of the error were the two problems I outlined previously: not enough pre-existing knowledge of Charles Dickens to be able to dismiss the wrong ideas, and not enough knowledge of the vocabulary to be able to properly understand what the text was saying. He must have found a website that explained how Dickens based parts of Pip's story on his own life, but then his weak understanding of the vocabulary being used meant he mistook Dickens for Pip.

I am not trying to say here that Internet research tasks are never good, any more than I would dismiss the use of dictionaries or print encyclopaedias. If research tasks have a tighter structure and they complement, rather than replace, the teacher's transmission of facts, then they can work. But that is not how they are being sold in the evidence and practice I outlined previously. Recall this history lesson praised by Ofsted:

Students in Year 9 were given the task of investigating changes in bombing strategy, comparing the First and Second World Wars. They devised their enquiries and structured them appropriately with individual guidance from the class teacher. Each student had her or his own laptop and used both academic and general interest websites to research data and find different interpretations. This valuable exercise led to some valid independent work. It was enhanced by the fact that, although students were given a broad framework and a key question which they were required to answer, the structure of the enquiry was not prescribed and the students were able to develop their own styles and structures.[19]

Perhaps the teacher did make sure that the class had enough prior information before the task began to make this activity worthwhile, but that is never made clear. Instead, it is suggested that the pupils are capable of finding all the data and interpretations they need for this very complex task on their own, on the Internet. This simply is not a realistic portrayal of how pupils learn complex material. Likewise, in this recommendation, Ofsted encourage all learning of new facts to come through looking them up on the Internet rather than teacher exposition:

> Staff who were unfamiliar with the new developments did not always capitalise on the pupils' improved learning skills, with the result that the pupils sometimes felt uncomfortable when they returned to what they described as the 'old type' of lessons. In one school, for example, the pupils had become used to ready access to their wireless laptops as part of a research-based approach to learning. This encouraged them to work independently and think more widely about aspects of their work. In lessons that did not use the same approach and relied heavily on exposition from the teacher, the pupils became restless and their concentration faltered. This highlighted the importance of ensuring that all staff understand the benefits of new approaches and are able to meet pupils' higher expectations.[20]

Again, we see the logical leap Ofsted make. They see one poor example of teacher exposition and assume from this that the problem is teacher exposition *per se* and that the answer is to abandon teacher exposition and replace it with Internet research. This is not the case. The solution to poor teacher exposition is better teacher exposition, not a complete absence of teacher exposition.

The other problem with some of the practical approaches we saw at the start of this chapter is that they assume research skills can be taught in the abstract. The RSA Opening Minds curriculum asks for a focus on developing research techniques, while Futurelab promote 'class discussion about sources of information and differing opinions' and 'the development of questioning skills'.[21]

I shall look more closely at the nature of skill development in the next chapter. But for now, what we need to know is that research skills are, on closer inspection, the function of large bodies of knowledge. Being a good researcher goes far beyond just being sceptical about what turns up on the first page of a Google search, and depends to a far greater extent on the knowledge you have about the topic being researched. Suppose someone gave me a computer with access to the Internet and asked me to find out which bowlers dismissed Don Bradman leg before wicket in Test matches. I do not know this, but given access to the Internet I could find out in seconds. I could go to the website www.cricinfo.com and search its Statsguru database of every Test match player and match.

Now, suppose someone asked me to find out which pitchers intentionally walked Chipper Jones more than once in major league baseball (MLB). I could have a go at randomly searching the Internet, but other than typing the query into Google I would not really know what to do. Using the exact phrase search option, I could type 'Chipper Jones', 'MLB' and 'intentionally walked' into Wikipedia and try and work out what these phrases were about, but I would still struggle to find the answer to the query. How is this possible? How can my Internet research skills be so good when it comes to one question, but so bad when it comes to another question that is fairly similar in terms of structure and difficulty?[22]

The difference is domain-specific knowledge. In both tasks, my knowledge of how the Internet worked was constant. But my domain-specific knowledge about the first question was very high, and this high level of knowledge allowed me to arrive quickly at the correct strategy for finding out the answer. I failed at the second task because I had barely any domain knowledge. To improve in the second task, I did not need tips on how to identify the correct source, use Google correctly and how to operate a database. I needed to know a lot more about baseball. I needed to know what the MLB was, what a pitcher was, who Chipper Jones was and what intentionally walking was. I devised this baseball question by asking a friend who knew a lot about both baseball and cricket to come up with a baseball question that was similar to the cricket one which I devised. He briefly explained to me what each term meant and how you would go about solving it. You would use a very similar process to the one I used for solving the cricket problem. There is a baseball reference website which includes historical records of many matches. You can construct queries which search its database. Even after he had shown me how he constructed the query, I still would not have been able to construct another, similar query myself. The only way I could become proficient at solving these types of research questions would be to know a lot more about baseball.

The reason why we can describe someone as having good research skills is that they have good general knowledge which makes most research tasks they encounter intelligible. I like to think I have good research skills, but as I have just showed, I can be easily stumped when presented with a research question I know nothing about.

You can only rely on being able to look something up when you know quite a bit about it to begin with. Being able to research something effectively is undoubtedly an important skill. But it is a skill that is dependent on broad knowledge. If we want our pupils to be able to look things up, then rather than focus solely on abstract and generic strategies, we need to make sure they have such broad knowledge, too. The same is true of many other important skills, such as creativity, analysis, problem-solving and even literacy. The best way to teach these skills will be the subject of the next chapter.

Notes

1   Quote Investigator. You don't have to know everything. You just have to know where to find it (2012), http://quoteinvestigator.com/2012/04/02/know-where-to-find/ (accessed 4 March 2013).
2   Wheeler, S. Content as curriculum? (2012), http://steve-wheeler.blogspot.co.uk/2011/12/content-as-curriculum.html (accessed 4 March 2013).
3   *Telegraph.* Learning by heart is 'pointless for Google generation' (2008), www.telegraph.co.uk/education/primaryeducation/3540852/Learning-by-heart-is-pointless-for-Google-generation.html (accessed 3 March 2013).
4   Association of Teachers and Lecturers. ATL conference 2012 – Cover story (2012), www.atl.org.uk/publications-and-resources/report/2012/2012-may-cover-story-conference.asp (accessed 4 March 2013).
5   *Telegraph.* Primary school league tables: Top head attacks 'pub quiz'-style schooling (2011), www.telegraph.co.uk/education/primaryeducation/8958808/Primary-school-league-tables-top-head-attacks-pub-quiz-style-schooling.html (accessed 4 March 2013).
6   Royal Society of Arts Opening Minds. RSA Opening Minds competence framework (2013), www.rsaopeningminds.org.uk/about-rsa-openingminds/competences/ (accessed 4 March 2013).
7   Ibid.
8   Payton, S. and Williamson, B. Enquiring minds: Innovative approaches to curriculum reform (2008), p. 33, http://archive.futurelab.org.uk/resources/documents/project_reports/Enquiring_Minds_year4_report.pdf (accessed 4 March 2013).
9   Ibid.
10 Office for Standards in Education, Children's Services and Skills. History for all: History in English schools 2007/10 (2011), p. 54, www.ofsted.gov.uk/resources/history-for-all (accessed 4 March 2013).
11 Office for Standards in Education, Children's Services and Skills. Geography: Learning to make a world of difference (2011), p. 16, www.ofsted.gov.uk/resources/geography-learning-make-world-of-difference (accessed 4 March 2013).
12 Office for Standards in Education, Children's Services and Skills. Making a mark: art, craft and design education 2008–11 (2012), p. 19, www.ofsted.gov.uk/resources/making-mark-art-craft-and-design-education-2008-11 (accessed 4 March 2013).
13 Office for Standards in Education, Children's Services and Skills. Curriculum innovation in schools (2008), pp. 15–16, www.ofsted.gov.uk/resources/curriculum-innovation-schools (accessed 4 March 2013).
14 Miller, G.A. and Gildea, P.M. How children learn words. *Scientific American* 1987; 257: 94–99.
15 Hirsch, E.D. You can always look it up … Or can you? *American Educator* Spring 2000 (2000), p. 2, www.aft.org/pdfs/americaneducator/spring2000/LookItUp Spring2000.pdf (accessed 4 March 2013).
16 Payton, S. and Williamson, B. Enquiring minds: Innovative approaches to curriculum reform (2008), p. 33, http://archive.futurelab.org.uk/resources/documents/project_reports/Enquiring_Minds_year4_report.pdf (accessed 4 March 2013).

17 Laufer, B. The lexical plight in second language reading: Words you don't know, words you think you know, and words you can't guess. In: Coady, J. and Huckin, T. (eds) *Second Language Vocabulary Acquisition: A Rationale for Pedagogy*. Cambridge: Cambridge University Press, 1997, pp. 20–34.

18 Hirsch, E.D. You can always look it up … Or can you? *American Educator* Spring 2000 (2000), p. 2, www.aft.org/pdfs/americaneducator/spring2000/LookItUp Spring2000.pdf (accessed 4 March 2013).

19 Office for Standards in Education, Children's Services and Skills. History for all: History in English schools 2007/10 (2011), p. 54, www.ofsted.gov.uk/resources/ history-for-all (accessed 4 March 2013).

20 Office for Standards in Education, Children's Services and Skills. Curriculum innovation in schools (2008), pp. 15–16, www.ofsted.gov.uk/resources/ curriculum-innovation-schools (accessed 4 March 2013).

21 Payton, S. and Williamson, B. Enquiring minds: Innovative approaches to curriculum reform (2008), p. 33, http://archive.futurelab.org.uk/resources/ documents/project_reports/Enquiring_Minds_year4_report.pdf (accessed 4 March 2013).

22 The answer to the cricket question can be found by searching Statsguru, http:// stats.espncricinfo.com/ci/engine/stats/index.html. The answer to the baseball question can be found on Baseball Reference.com, http://tiny.cc/kofjtw (both accessed 6 March 2013).

Myth 5

We should teach transferable skills

Where is the evidence that people believe this and that it has affected education policy and classroom practice?

Theoretical evidence

In Chapter 3, we encountered a myth that told us knowledge was constantly being changed. In Chapter 4, we encountered a myth that gave a solution to the myth of Chapter 3. Do not teach knowledge; instead, you can rely on your pupils looking it up. If you follow this logic, it leaves you with a bit of a problem. Having removed the need to teach knowledge, you then have to fill up the time pupils spend in school with something else. What is it to be? This chapter provides one of the most common answers: teach transferable skills. Teach pupils the how, not the what. Teach them how to solve problems, how to analyse, how to think critically, how to evaluate. Teach them how to apply these important skills to whatever content they might encounter, now and later in life. Above all, teach them how to learn, because if you teach pupils how to learn, then it does not matter how fast knowledge changes. They will always be able to learn whatever it is they need at that present moment. As David Miliband noted in 2003, one of the most important functions of twenty-first century teaching is 'learning how to learn in preparation for a lifetime of change'.[1]

For Professor Guy Claxton, too, it is learning how to learn which is particularly important. Claxton is a psychologist who has written a number of books about education and about the importance of 'learning power'. He is the Co-Director of the Centre for Real-World Learning and Professor of the Learning Sciences at the University of Winchester. His work on 'building learning power' is referred to and praised in a report by Ofsted. [2] For him, 'it is the job of education to strengthen their [young people's] ability to be good choosers, skilful problem-solvers and powerful learners'.[3] This is because whilst specific knowledge and skills may become outdated quickly, 'the generic ability to learn has no use-by date at all'.[4] Pupils who don't have the capacity to learn new things are 'illearnerate'; therefore, 'more fundamental even than the concern with literacy and numeracy is the need to protect and develop young people's "learnacy"'.[5] As this would suggest, Claxton agrees with much of the logic we saw in the previous two chapters; namely, that the nature of modern technological change means we cannot reliably teach our pupils knowledge:

> There are two good reasons for reconfiguring 21st century education: economic and personal. The well-rehearsed economic argument says that knowledge is changing so fast that we cannot give young people what they will need to know, because we do not know what it will be. Instead we should be helping them to develop supple and nimble minds, so that they will be able to learn whatever they need to. If we can achieve that, we will have a world-class workforce comprising people who are innovative and resourceful.[6]

The aim is for pupils 'to develop supple and nimble minds'. Claxton develops this metaphor, of the mind as a muscle, at length. Education is about exercising important mental muscle groups:

> Which mental muscle groups are specifically exercised by maths, or history or music? Can favourite topics defend their place if looked at in this light?[7]

The metaphor of mental muscles makes it clear that skills are transferable and teachable. You can use a real muscle to pick up a bag of shopping or a pile of books; it is also possible to exercise a real muscle and to improve its generic performance. So the metaphor of mental muscles suggests that we have the capacity to teach and learn generic skills such as learning, creativity or problem-solving. In the practice section of this chapter I shall look at how Claxton suggests we should teach these generic skills.

The RSA Opening Minds curriculum follows a similar logic. We have already seen what their five core competences are. The justification for this is as follows:

> A competence-based approach enables students not just to acquire subject knowledge but to understand, use and apply it within the context of their wider learning and life. It also offers students a more holistic and coherent way of learning which allows them to make connections and apply knowledge across different subject areas.[8]

In their report on the curriculum, the Association of Teachers and Lecturers state the following:

> Rote learning of facts must give way to nurturing through education of essential transferable skills that enable the next generation to navigate the information age.[9]

Yet again, we see the opposition between learning facts and learning skills. Ultimately, most of the theories about teaching transferable skills end up reproducing this dichotomy and assuming that transferable skills negate the need to teach facts.

Modern practice

When we consider how this theory works in practice, we see that many of the attempts to teach transferable skills involve a reduction in the time spent teaching subjects and an increase in the time given to projects. I shall deal with the subject/project debate in the next chapter, but for now let us look at some of the practical ways that transferable skills are taught, whether it is via projects or in other ways.

We saw in Chapter 1 that the designers of the current National Curriculum (NC) deliberately reduced the amount of content included in it. Many schools have used this as an opportunity to reorganise their school day to promote the teaching of transferable skills. Instead of organising the curriculum around subjects, they have chosen to organise it around skills instead. There are a couple of important external agencies that have helped with this approach. The RSA's Opening Minds curriculum, which we looked at in Chapter 3, is probably the most prominent example. Campion School in Northamptonshire introduced Opening Minds in 2004 and recorded their experiences as part of the National Teacher Research Panel:

> The OM projects have been mapped against the National Curriculum but with a focus on the skills rather than the content. It is evident when the National Curriculum is scrutinised in this way that there is much similarity in subject requirements, e.g. all subject areas require students to evaluate, describe, explain etc. Students need these and many other strategies to be successful in life.[10]

Campion School are right, of course: as we saw in Chapter 1, close scrutiny of the NC does reveal that there is much similarity in the subject requirements of the NC. Indeed, the NC was designed to promote this kind of approach.

The aim of Campion School's reforms was to promote the learning of transferable skills:

- Help to develop transferable skills and competencies such as literacy, numeracy and ICT in the Key Stage 3 curriculum.
- Embed Learning to Learn and Emotional Intelligence into the curriculum.[11]

Certain subjects were merged into one and taught as projects. The aim is for 80 per cent of curriculum time to be taken up by Opening Minds and for this time to be spent doing Opening Minds projects. There are six projects each year, of which the following five are examples: Smart Brain (the first project and based around Learning to Learn), Breaking News, Global Affairs, It's Not Fair and Time.[12] Unfortunately, further detail on exactly what is studied in specific lessons is not available.

While Opening Minds promotes this kind of approach, so too do a series of popular teaching guides by Chris Quigley.[13] These resources allow you to convert the Key Stage 1 (KS1) and 2 (KS2) NC skills into six half-termly themes, or projects. They provide a grid that lists the NC subject skills. Schools can then teach projects and map the skills across from the curriculum to the project. As the skills are the only statutory part of the KS1 and KS2 curriculum, this approach is permitted within the NC.

In fact, this approach is actively encouraged by Ofsted. In a very recent publication, they praise a school for an 'innovative, cross-curricular topic approach' which is very similar in structure to the Opening Minds one.[14] In a 2008 report into curriculum innovation that is generally positive, they note that schools took four main approaches to curriculum innovation:

- curriculum delivery through themes or interdisciplinary links rather than discrete subjects;
- flexible use of curriculum time;
- alternative curriculum pathways;
- a concentration on developing learning skills.[15]

The first and last of these involve the kind of innovation we have been discussing. One example of innovation from this report shows the similarities to Opening Minds:

> During Year 7, every pupil completed six projects, each lasting half a term, on the themes of 'journeys', 'identity', 'positive images', 'art attack', 'survival' and 'the power and the glory'. These drew on geography, history, religious education, dance, drama, art, and personal, social and health education. The pupils were able to assess their development against defined competencies, weekly or in individual lessons. As a result, they gained an understanding of their strengths and weaknesses which provided a powerful stimulus to learning and raising standards.[16]

Not all approaches to transferable skills involve completely getting rid of subjects. In *Building Learning Power in Action*, Guy Claxton and two collaborators give a number of examples of activities that could be introduced to subject lessons to help pupils improve their ability to learn and develop their skills. For example, to teach the skill of imagining through the subject of science, they recommend the following:

Students use role play to understand complex moral issues better. They imagine and enact the emotions, perceptions and behaviour of people involved, as a starting point for discussion.[17]

To teach the skill of imagining through the subject of geography, they recommend the following activity:

Students lie on the ground, look at sky and relax. They observe detail in the clouds, then close their eyes to imagine how the sky changes as a storm approaches. They relate their imagined changes to further knowledge as they acquire it.[18]

However, there are a huge number of activities and lessons involving pupils reflecting on learning which do not really fit into any subject lesson. For example, the book recommends that:

Pupils create images of aspects of being a good learner: a beehive represents buzzing with ideas; a toolkit indicates the range of skills needed to be a good learner. They match pictures of themselves and others to images on displays to show learning behaviours they have noted.[19]

Reflection on learning seems to be an essential part of many lessons which try to directly teach transferable skills. At Campion School they run a discrete lesson on learning every two weeks:

The content of the learning to learn course includes areas such as:

- All about the brain.
- How emotions affect the brain and how to control your temper.
- We investigate the nature of intelligence.
- The multiple intelligence model and how to use it to break down barriers to learning.
- Learning styles.
- We assess left and right brain preferences as well as visual auditory and kinaesthetic styles of learning.

The focus here is on how to use your whole brain for smarter working. Emotional Intelligence. We look at what other qualities are needed in life to be a success, as defined by Daniel Goleman – persistence, optimism, empathy, mood control, self awareness and deferred gratification. We attempt to teach these qualities explicitly and suggest that students can develop these qualities – and must if they want to succeed. We also work on thinking skills and research skills. It is taught by specialists. That is by teachers who have completed our school-based MBA module on the management of effective teaching and learning which explores the theories of accelerated learning in some depth. Lessons include the use of music (brain-wave friendly of course) and brain gym at 20 minute intervals. They always begin with a note in the learning log. The lessons are underpinned by an encouragement to engage in metacognition – standing back from the way you think and understanding it.[20]

What Campion School call 'metacognition' is a popular approach. For example, the 'reciprocal reading' programme uses metacognition to help pupils learn to read. It is a pupil-led programme that involves pupils following four strategies as they are reading to try to improve their comprehension. After they have read a segment of text, they follow these four strategies to make sure they have understood: question, summarise, clarify and predict.[21] Ofsted's most recent advice on literacy recommends a similar approach to the direct teaching of literacy skills:

> Too few schools currently develop reading skills effectively across the curriculum. Inspectors rarely see the direct teaching of skills such as skimming, scanning and reading for detail (including on the internet); using the index and glossary; identifying key points and making notes; summarising; or using more than one source.[22]

To sum up, many schools have reorganised their curriculum to teach transferable skills. One of the most popular ways to do this is to teach more project-based and thematic lessons.

Why is this a myth?

The truth at the heart of this myth is that of course we do want our pupils to be able to transfer what they know and can do to new and unfamiliar situations. That is one of the goals of teaching. Where it goes wrong is that it claims you need specific lessons focused on abstract skill acquisition to develop these abilities.

As we have already seen, knowledge and skills are intertwined, and they are intertwined to such an extent that it is not really possible to separate out skills in isolation and teach them on their own. And when you analyse fully the claims that are made by the proponents of transferable skills, this should be apparent. Campion School noted, correctly, that the skills for the different NC subjects were all very similar. And so they are. But does this really mean that you can teach them in a similar fashion? It is true that you need to analyse tough maths problems, and that you need to analyse difficult historical questions. Is there a way of teaching a lesson that helps develop the analysis skill for both? It is true that we want pupils to be able to communicate scientific facts fluently, and that we also want them to communicate literary facts fluently. But is there one all-purpose communication strategy that will develop expertise in both?

The answer is no. Dan Willingham shows that we have a common misconception of how the mind works. We tend to think that the brain works like a calculator – that it can perform a certain operation on certain data, regardless of what the data are. If you can perform a certain operation on one set of data, then, like a calculator, you can perform that operation on any set of data. This is of course the theory underpinning much of what we saw on the Opening Minds curriculum; as they said at Campion School, it was easy to combine all the NC subjects together because the skills required were so similar. But this is not how the brain works:

> But the human mind does not work that way. When we learn to think critically about, say, the start of the Second World War, it does not mean we can also think critically about a chess game, or about the current situation in the Middle East, or even about the start of the American Revolutionary War. Critical thinking processes are tied to background knowledge (although they become much less so when we become quite experienced, as I describe in Chapter Six). The conclusion from this work in cognitive science is straightforward: we must ensure that students acquire background knowledge parallel with practicing critical thinking skills.[23]

Very few of the lessons we saw previously took the time to make sure that pupils did acquire background knowledge.

Lots of the interesting research on this topic has been done with chess players. One much-cited experiment dates from 1946 and was conducted by Adriaan de Groot, a Dutch chess master and psychologist. It is described here by Herbert Simon and William Chase:

> He [de Groot] displayed a chess position to his subjects for a very brief period of time (2 to 10 seconds) and then asked them to reconstruct the position from memory. These positions were from actual master games, but games unknown to his subjects. The results were dramatic. Grandmasters and masters were able to reproduce, with almost perfect accuracy (about 93% correct), positions containing about 25 pieces. There was a quite sharp drop-off in performance somewhere near the boundary between players classified as masters, who did nearly as well as grandmasters, and players classified as experts, who did significantly worse (about 72%). Good amateurs (Class A players in the American rating scheme) could replace only about half the pieces in the same positions, and novice players (from our own experiments) could recall only about eight pieces (about 33%).[24]

Several years later, Simon and Chase repeated de Groot's experiment and got the same result. But they went on to add a crucial control experiment:

We went one step further: we took the same pieces that were used in the previous experiment, but now constructed random positions with them. Under the same conditions, all players, from master to novice, recalled only about three or four pieces on the average – performing significantly more poorly here than the novice did on the real positions.[25]

This is a famous and significant experiment showing the importance of long-term memory to cognition. Chess is supposed to be a game of pure reasoning, a game where strong and abstract 'mental muscles' separate the best players from the weakest. But in actual fact, one of the most important differences between the best players and the weakest players is the knowledge they have of typical chess positions. Chess turns out to be highly knowledge-bound. The same is true of other domains, as Hirsch explains:

> This experiment has been duplicated in several different laboratories, and structurally in several other fields, including algebra, physics and medicine, always with the same striking results. When the configuration of a task is significantly changed, past skills are not transferred to the new problem. In normal circumstances, of course, elements from past problems appear in present ones, and experts perform well with duplicated elements. But beyond similar or analogous circumstances, skill is not transferred.[26]

Building on his experiment, Simon suggested that expert chess players have between 10,000 and 100,000 chunks of chess positions stored in long-term memory.[27] That is where a grand master's chess expertise derives from, not from an abstract reasoning muscle. Similarly, the idea that teaching pupils strategies or tips for analysing or thinking critically will allow them to exercise their analysis or critical thinking muscle is flawed.

So how do we explain the fact that some adults clearly do have good general thinking skills? And how can we ensure all pupils are able to develop such skills? The answer to both questions is knowledge:

> Effective people have gained 21st-century skills because they have domain knowledge in a wide range of domains. This turns out to be the only answer consistent with a massive body of evidence ... 21st-century skills ... are knowledge based. Knowledge is skill: skill knowledge. A high score on a general knowledge test tends to correlate with 21st-century skills because the *only* reliable foundation for such skills is the possession of wide-ranging knowledge across many domains.[28]

Hirsch is right to note that knowledge is skill. This can seem counter-intuitive. When we use the words 'skill' and 'knowledge' in everyday contexts, they clearly mean something different. The word 'skill' does very clearly describe a phenomenon we all understand. If we describe someone as being skilled at solving mathematical problems, we obviously do not just mean that they know their times tables and lists of formulae. We mean that they can manipulate the knowledge they have and apply it to problems they have not seen before.

But whilst the word 'skill' is very useful at describing a reality, it is much less useful at providing us with analysis of that reality. Here is what Herbert Simon says about the ability of words to confuse rather than explain:

> The magic of words is such that, when we are unable to explain a phenomenon, we sometimes find a name for it as Molière's physician 'explained' the effects of opium by its dormitive property. So we 'explain' superior problem-solving skill by calling it 'talent', 'intuition', 'judgment' and 'imagination'.[29]

The same is true of the word 'skill'. It is excellent at describing a phenomenon we all recognise. But it is less good at explaining how we have acquired or can acquire that property. To describe someone as a good solver of maths problems may be true, and useful. But to attempt to explain that she is good at maths problems because of her high levels of mathematical skill is less useful. This explanation merely begs the question. Simon goes on to say:

> Behind such words, however, there usually lies a reality we must discover if we are to understand expert performance. One label often applied to persons skilful in solving physics and engineering problems is 'physical intuition'. A person with good physical intuition can often solve difficult problems rapidly and without much conscious deliberation about a plan of attack. It just 'occurs to him (or her)' that applying the principle of conservation of momentum will cause the answer to fall out, or that a term in kinetic energy can be ignored because it will be small in comparison with other terms in an equation. But admitting the reality of physical intuition is simply the prelude to demanding an explanation for it. How does it operate, and how can it be acquired?[30]

So, what does cause high levels of mathematical skill, or any other skill? This is the question that Simon devoted a great deal of his research to answering. In this article, he concludes with the following:

> In every domain that has been explored, considerable knowledge has been found to be an essential prerequisite to expert skill. Our growing understanding of an expert's knowledge and the kinds of processes an expert uses when solving problems enables us to begin to explore the learning processes needed to acquire suitable knowledge and problem-solving processes. We have no reason to suppose, however, that one day people will be able to become painlessly and instantly expert. The extent of the knowledge an expert must be able to call upon is demonstrably

large, and everything we know about human learning processes suggests
that, even at their most efficient, those processes must be long exercised.
Although we have a reasonable basis for hope that we may find ways to
make learning processes more efficient, we should not expect to produce
the miracle of effortless learning.[31]

A quotation from the Simon essay on chess expertise is also relevant:

> The question is: how does one become a master in the first place? The
> answer is practice – thousands of hours of practice ... Early in practice,
> these move sequences are arrived at by slow, conscious heuristic search –
> 'If I take that piece, then he takes this piece ...' – but with practice, the
> initial condition is seen as a pattern, quickly and unconsciously, and the
> plausible move comes almost automatically. Such a learning process takes
> time – years – to build the thousands of familiar chunks needed for master
> level chess. Clearly, practice also interacts with talent, and certain
> combinations of basic cognitive capacities may have special relevance for
> chess. But there is no evidence that masters demonstrate more than above-
> average competence on basic intellectual factors; their talents are chess
> specific (although World Champion caliber grandmasters may possess truly
> exceptional talents along certain dimensions). The acquisition of chess skill
> depends, in large part, on building up recognition memory.[32]

We've already seen Anderson say something similar:

> All that there is to intelligence is the simple accrual and tuning of many
> small units of knowledge that in total produce complex cognition. The
> whole is no more than the sum of its parts, but it has a lot of parts.[33]

What we see, therefore, is that the phenomenon of skill which we observe all
the time is explained by the knowledge we have in long-term memory and the
practice we have at retrieving that knowledge from memory. Note, too, that
what is important is the practice we have at retrieving that specific piece of
knowledge, not the generic ability to retrieve any piece of knowledge.

Very often, I hear people argue that the distinction between knowledge and
skills is a false dichotomy. As we've seen, this is the case. It is wrong to conceive
of knowledge and skill as polar opposites. However, I then often see people
conclude from this that we should teach both skills and knowledge. This is not
the case. What Simon shows us is that it isn't really possible to teach skills in this
abstract fashion. We achieve skilled performance through committing knowledge
to long-term memory and practising using it. Once we've recognised that the
distinction between knowledge and skills is a false dichotomy, the practical
conclusion we should draw is this: if pupils commit knowledge to memory and
practise retrieving it from memory, that will cause skilled performance.

It may be argued that I am splitting hairs here and this is a minor semantic point. And it is indeed true that there are doubtless many people who talk about teaching skills who nevertheless are in fact teaching the building blocks of knowledge that will cause skilled performance. But the reason why I think it's worthwhile dwelling on this is that too often that is not the case. Too often, as we have seen in the first part of this chapter, this semantic point is the root of actual bad practice. If you think that your teaching time should be completely devoted to teaching skills, or if you think that it should be divided in some kind of proportion between teaching knowledge and teaching skills, the time that is given over to teaching skills is devoted to practice that won't actually improve skills. For example, as we have seen, many theorists recommend teaching generic reading skill by getting pupils to skim texts, scan them and find the main idea. But these tactics have a very limited benefit because reading is not a generic skill. Reading depends on knowledge, so if you want to improve your pupils' reading skill, you would be better off spending your time on vocabulary acquisition or indeed teaching pupils knowledge from other subjects. Indeed, most of the lessons described in the previous evidence section involve pupils engaged in activities that claim to build skill, but which do not build the knowledge necessary for skill. When you realise how important it is for pupils to build broad general knowledge, the opportunity costs of such lessons become frighteningly apparent. Time spent imagining how to design a role play about complex moral issues in science is time not spent actually learning about atoms, compounds, mixtures and the states of matter. Time spent drawing pictures of beehives buzzing with idea-bees is time not spent learning important historical facts that allow pupils to create a chronological schema. Time spent on activities that are supposed to promote transferable skills is time not spent learning knowledge that will actually build transferable skills.

It is also worrying that some of the practice I described previously buys into discredited, pseudo-scientific notions about learning. In her description of Campion School's Learning to Learn module, Jackie Beere says that the pupils start by doing Brain Gym, and go on to work out their favoured learning style – visual, auditory or kinaesthetic. Opening Minds also includes learning styles as one of its key competences. Both Brain Gym and learning styles have been completely discredited.[34] There is no evidence supporting either concept. I did not include them in my list of myths because they have been so thoroughly and persuasively debunked elsewhere. It is worrying to see that such ideas are still being peddled despite this. But it is perhaps not surprising that they exist alongside the myths I am outlining.

The same principles apply to reading. We tend to think of reading as an all-purpose skill that can be applied to any piece of text, and we saw Ofsted's recommendations for the direct teaching of reading skills. In actual fact, good readers are those who tend to know a little bit about a lot. Their wide general knowledge enables them to be able to read a wide range of texts effectively.

Likewise, even supposedly good readers struggle when the topic of the text changes to something they know little about; consider how most English people would struggle when presented with the sports pages of an American newspaper. Part of this is to do with unfamiliar vocabulary, of course. But it goes much deeper than that. Reading a text does not just involve knowing what the words mean. It involves understanding the context of those words and the concepts they refer to. As we read, we use the knowledge in our long-term memory – the schemata I talked about in Chapter 1 – to make sense of the words. If I read the word *train* in a bridal magazine, I use a very different schema than if I read the word *train* in a railway magazine. If I read the word *Essex* in a discussion of Elizabeth, Ireland and Drake, I use a very different schema than if I read the word *Essex* in a discussion of white stilettos, reality TV shows and nightclubs. Or take the following sentence:

Jones sacrificed and knocked in a run.[35]

Most English people will know the meaning of every word in that sentence, but they will be unable to understand at all what it means. That is because 'to understand this sentence about Jones and his sacrifice, you need a wealth of relevant background knowledge that goes beyond vocabulary and syntax – relevant knowledge that is far broader than the words of the sentence'.[36] If you read that sentence and did not understand it, applying the four reciprocal reading strategies is not going to help you very much. To understand that sentence you do not need to improve your reading skill; you need more knowledge.

An interesting experiment by Recht and Leslie proves this point.[37] It is described here by Dan Willingham:

A clever study on this point was conducted with junior high school students. Half were good readers and half were poor readers, according to standard reading tests. The researchers asked the students to read a story that described half an innings of a baseball game. As they read, the students were periodically stopped and asked to show that they understood what was happening in the story by using a model of a baseball field and players. The interesting thing about this study was that some of the students knew a lot about baseball and some knew just a little. (The researcher made sure that everyone could comprehend individual actions, for example, what happened when a player got a double.) The dramatic finding … was that the students' knowledge of baseball determined how much they understood of the story. Whether they were 'good readers' or 'bad readers' didn't matter nearly as much as what they knew.[38]

In the words of Recht and Leslie, 'the finding that summarisation of poor readers with high knowledge of baseball was far superior to that of good readers without such knowledge demonstrates the powerful effect of knowledge on memory'.[39] Many other experiments bear out this finding.[40]

The reason why so many of these examples involve sports knowledge is that sports knowledge is the kind of knowledge that otherwise well-informed people might not have. Someone who does not like sport and listens in to a conversation on sport will often remark that it is like hearing another language. This is the position many of our pupils are in when hearing or reading about a whole range of topics. It is hard to imagine what this is like if you do have this knowledge. As Hirsch says, this kind of general knowledge is like oxygen.[41] It is vitally important, but we only notice it when it is not there. In normal circumstances, we take it for granted. I think that many educated people underestimate how much knowledge they have, and overestimate how much knowledge children have. The point of using the baseball examples is to try to expose our hidden dependency on knowledge. It is to help us realise what it is like if you do not have knowledge. Everything appears strange and confusing.

Here is an example of this from my own experience. A few years ago I gave two groups of year 11 pupils an exam past paper. They were the top two sets. All 55 pupils were predicted C grades or above, and all 55 did indeed go on to get C grades or above. They had all been consistently working close to their target grades when I gave them this past paper. It consisted of an unseen extract from a short story by Arthur C. Clarke.[42] The story is about a man who is the last human left in a futuristic London that has been submerged in ice and snow. He is constantly hearing loud noises from the North. He knows that if men were coming to rescue him, they would be more likely to come from the South, but he hopes against hope anyway. The punchline is that the noise turns out to be a glacier.

As I read it in preparation for the lesson, I guessed what would happen – no one would get a very good mark because no one knew what a glacier was and proper understanding of the story depended on this. I was right. Out of the 55 pupils, not one fully understood what a glacier was and hence could fully understand what the story was about. Some clearly had vague knowledge that a glacier involved ice. Many of them thought that the glacier was some kind of tribe or army advancing from the North. They were supposed to spend an hour doing the paper in silence. Both were well-behaved classes who took activities like this seriously, but about 20 minutes into the task I heard groans and moans and complaints about how difficult it was. Some of the pupils were simply unable to answer any of the questions. They just did not understand what was happening. All the painstaking exam strategies and reading techniques I had prepped them with over the previous months were useless. They could not 'find the main idea' because they just did not know what it was. 'Rereading carefully' and 'underlining words you are not sure about' were equally ineffective. These pupils were not stupid. They simply lacked a crucial piece of knowledge. Their experience was not unusual. The examiners' report on the exam stated:

Given the current interest in environmental issues, and the popularity of a particular type of film and television programme, it was surprising that a number of candidates seemed unaware of what a glacier is and some seemed to be convinced that the glaciers were some sort of tribe, presumably advancing from somewhere in the north.[43]

Incidentally, this is another example of an influential educationalist outsourcing the responsibility for teaching knowledge to the media and assuming that knowledge acquisition is not the responsibility of schools and teachers.

If you consider the headlines of any broadsheet newspaper, you will see just how much knowledge they assume their readers have. Here is the first paragraph of a news article from the online edition of the *Guardian* newspaper, dated 5 December 2011:

Germany and France have struck a grand bargain that they hope will save the euro, burying their differences over a rigorous new regime to drive down eurozone debt and restore market confidence in the battered single currency.[44]

Consider how much knowledge that one sentence requires. First of all, it requires both a geographical and a political understanding of Germany and France. Knowing what the words *grand* and *bargain* mean individually will not tell you the meaning of *grand bargain*. The same is true of *market* and *confidence* in *market confidence*. *Eurozone debt* requires knowledge of geography, economics and politics. Those are just the obvious points. Clearly, understanding of this passage would be helped by a general understanding of modern European politics, history and culture. The same is true of most news articles in broadsheet newspapers. They assume a lot of information on behalf of their readers. If we want our pupils to be able to understand such articles – hardly an unreasonable aim – we will need to teach such knowledge. Teaching all-purpose or generic reading strategies is simply not enough.

To sum up, we are again met with the paradox of so many of these myths. The aim of teaching transferable skills is for pupils to develop effective, all-purpose skills. But the methods used by the advocates of transferable skills ensure that their pupils will not develop such skills. That is because these methods systematically misrepresent the very nature of skills and their knowledge-bound character. In the next chapter, I shall examine such methods in more detail and show why they are unsuccessful.

Notes

1   *Guardian.* Teaching in the 21st century (2003), www.guardian.co.uk/ education/2003/jan/08/itforschools.schools (accessed 4 March 2013).

2   Claxton, G. *Building Learning Power: Helping Young People Become Better Learners.*
     Bristol: TLO, 2002; Office for Standards in Education, Children's Services and
     Skills. Geography: Learning to make a world of difference (2011), p. 34, www.
     ofsted.gov.uk/resources/geography-learning-make-world-of-difference (accessed
     4 March 2013).

3   Claxton, G. Expanding the capacity to learn: A new end for education? (2006), p. 2,
     www.guyclaxton.com/documents/New/BERA%20Keynote%20Final.pdf
     (accessed 4 March 2013).

4   Ibid.

5   Claxton, G. Learning to learn: A key goal in a 21st century curriculum (2013), p. 1,
     www.cumbria.ac.uk/Public/Education/Documents/Research/ESCalateDocuments/
     QCAArticlebyGuyClaxton.pdf (accessed 4 March 2013).

6   Ibid.

7   Ibid., p. 2.

8   Royal Society of Arts Action and Research Centre. Opening minds (2013), www.
     thersa.org/action-research-centre/education/practical-projects/opening-minds
     (accessed 4 March 2013).

9   Association of Teachers and Lecturers. Subject to change: New thinking on the
     curriculum (2007), p. 9, www.atl.org.uk/Images/Subject%20to%20change.pdf
     (accessed 3 March 2013).

10   National Teacher Research Panel: Engaging Teacher Expertise. Opening Minds: A
     competency-based curriculum for the twenty first century (2006), p. 3, www.ntrp.
     org.uk/sites/all/documents/HBSummary.pdf (accessed 4 March 2013).

11   Ibid.

12   Boyle, H. Opening minds: A competency based curriculum at Campion School
     (2007), www.teachingexpertise.com/articles/opening-minds-a-competency-based-
     curriculum-at-campion-school-2512 (accessed 4 March 2013).

13   Chris Quigley Education Limited. Key skills in National Curriculum subjects
     (2011), www.chrisquigley.co.uk/products_keyskills.php (accessed 4 March 2013).

14   Office for Standards in Education, Children's Services and Skills. Good practice
     resource – Innovative curriculum design to raise attainment: Middlestone Moor
     Primary School (2012), p. 2, www.ofsted.gov.uk/resources/good-practice-
     resource-innovative-curriculum-design-raise-attainment-middlestone-moor-
     primary-school (accessed 7 March 2013).

15   Office for Standards in Education, Children's Services and Skills. Curriculum
     innovation in schools (2008), p. 8, www.ofsted.gov.uk/resources/curriculum-
     innovation-schools (accessed 4 March 2013).

16   Ibid., pp. 9 and 10.

17   Gornall, S., Chambers, M. and Claxton, G. *Building Learning Power in Action.*
     Bristol: TLO Ltd, 2005, p. 24.

18   Ibid.

19   Ibid., p. 38.

20   Independent Thinking Ltd. Lessons in learning to learn (2013), www.independent
     thinking.co.uk/Cool+Stuff/Articles/129.aspx (accessed 4 March 2013).

21   Brown, A.L., Palincsar, A.S, University of Illinois at Urbana-Champaign, et al.
     *Reciprocal Teaching of Comprehension Strategies: A Natural History of One Program for
     Enhancing Learning (Technical Report No. 334).* Cambridge, MA: Bolt Beranek and
     Newman Inc., 1985.

22 Office for Standards in Education, Children's Services and Skills. Moving English forward: Action to raise standards in English (2012), p. 30, www.ofsted.gov.uk/resources/moving-english-forward (accessed 4 March 2013).

23 Willingham, D.T. *Why Don't Students Like School?* San Francisco: Jossey-Bass, 2009, p. 29.

24 Simon, H. and Chase, W. Skill in chess. *American Scientist* 1973; 61: 394–403, p. 395; de Groot, A.D. *Thought and Choice in Chess.* The Hague: Mouton, 1978.

25 Simon, H. and Chase, W. Skill in chess. *American Scientist* 1973; 61: 394–403, p. 395.

26 Hirsch, E.D. *Cultural Literacy: What Every American Needs to Know.* Boston: Houghton Mifflin, 1987, p. 61.

27 Simon, H.A. and Gilmartin, K. A simulation of memory for chess positions. *Cognitive Psychology* 1973; 5: 29–46.

28 Hirsch, E.D. The 21st century skills movement. *Common Core News* (2009), http://commoncore.org/pressrelease-04.php (accessed 4 March 2013).

29 Larkin, J., McDermott, J., Simon, D.P. and Simon, H.A. Expert and novice performance in solving physics problems. *Science*, 1980; 208(4450), 1335–1342, p. 1335.

30 Ibid.

31 Ibid, p. 1342.

32 Simon, H. and Chase, W. Skill in chess. *American Scientist* 1973; 61: 394–403, p. 403.

33 Anderson, J.R. ACT: A simple theory of complex cognition. *American Psychologist* 1996; 51: 355–365.

34 For a summary of Brain Gym, see Goldacre, B. *Bad Science.* London: Fourth Estate, 2008, pp. 13–20. For a summary of learning styles, see Willingham, D.T. *Why Don't Students Like School?* San Francisco: Jossey-Bass, 2009, pp. 147–168. For further information on Brain Gym, see Hyatt, K.J. Brain Gym® – Building stronger brains or wishful thinking? *Remedial and Special Education* 2007; 28: 117–124. For further information on learning styles, see Coffield, F. Learning and Skills Research Centre (Great Britain), et al. *Should we be Using Learning Styles? What Research has to say to Practice.* London: Learning and Skills Research Centre, 2004; Sharp, J.G., Bowker, R. and Byrne, J. VAK or VAK-uous? Towards the trivialisation of learning and the death of scholarship. *Research Papers in Education* 2008; 23: 293–314; Kratzig, G.P. and Arbuthnott, K.D. Perceptual learning style and learning proficiency: A test of the hypothesis. *Journal of Educational Psychology* 2006; 98: 238–246.

35 Hirsch, E.D. *The Knowledge Deficit.* Boston: Houghton Mifflin, 2006, p. 68.

36 Ibid.

37 Recht, D.R. and Leslie, L. Effect of prior knowledge on good and poor readers' memory of text. *Journal of Educational Psychology* 1988; 80: 16–20.

38 Willingham, D.T. *Why Don't Students Like School?* San Francisco: Jossey-Bass, 2009, p. 35.

39 Recht, D.R. and Leslie, L. Effect of prior knowledge on good and poor readers' memory of text. *Journal of Educational Psychology* 1988; 80: 16–20, p. 19.

40 See, for example, Pearson, P.D. The effect of background knowledge on young children's comprehension of explicit and implicit information. *Journal of Reading Behavior* 1979; 11: 201–209; Taft, M.L. and Leslie, L. The effects of prior knowledge

and oral reading accuracy on miscues and comprehension. *Journal of Reading Behavior* 1985; 17: 163–179; Taylor, B.M. Good and poor readers' recall of familiar and unfamiliar text. *Journal of Reading Behavior* 1979; 11: 375–380; McNamara, D. and Kintsch, W. Learning from texts: Effect of prior knowledge and text coherence. *Discourse Processes* 1996; 22: 247–288; Caillies, S., Denhière, G. and Kintsch, W. The effect of prior knowledge on understanding from text: Evidence from primed recognition. *European Journal of Cognitive Psychology* 2002; 14: 267–286.

41 Hirsch, E.D. *Cultural Literacy: What Every American Needs to Know.* Boston: Houghton Mifflin, 1987, p. 19.

42 Welsh Joint Education Committee (CBAC). GCSE, 150/05, English Higher Tier Paper 1, A.M. Tuesday, 6 June 2006 (2006). This exam paper is no longer available online, although the examiners' report on it is (see below). The exam extract was taken from the short story 'The Forgotten Enemy' by Arthur C. Clarke which can be found in *Reach for Tomorrow*. New York: Ballantine Books, 1956.

43 Welsh Joint Education Committee (CBAC). GCSE Examiners' Report Summer 2006: English & English Literature (2006), p. 19, www.wjec.co.uk/uploads/publications/g-xr-english-s-06.pdf (accessed 4 March 2013).

44 *Guardian.* Eurozone crisis: Germany and France agree rescue package (2011), www.guardian.co.uk/business/2011/dec/05/germany-france-euro-merkel-sarkozy (accessed 4 March 2013).

Myth 6

Projects and activities are the best way to learn

Where is the evidence that people believe this and that it has affected education policy and classroom practice?

Theoretical evidence

In Chapter 2, we saw how many theorists and educationalists dislike teacher-directed methods. In this chapter, I shall look more closely at the main methods they advocate instead, and at why such methods are less successful.

The main methods advocated by theorists who reject teacher-directed learning tend to involve projects and activities. The aim of such activities is to replicate real-world problems rather than force pupils to learn through an artificial school-based structure. In the real world, problems do not come neatly wrapped in a box marked *Maths* or *English*. They require you to pull together knowledge and skills from across different domains. And yet, the subject-based teaching system denies pupils the chance to solve these real-world problems. Subjects become silos and pupils are unable to develop a holistic understanding of the world. Steve Wheeler says:

> We need to move with the times, and many schools are still lagging woefully behind the current needs of society. Why do we compartmentalise our subjects in silos? When will we begin to realise that all subjects have overlaps and commonalities, and children need to understand these overlaps to obtain a clear and full picture of their world. Without holistic forms of education, no-one is going to make the link between science and maths, or understand how art or music have influenced history.[1]

Pupils taught like this are unable to develop the independence they will need to tackle real-life problems. University professors frequently warn that many of their students are unaccustomed to independent learning. They have become so used to being spoon-fed knowledge at school that they are unable to learn independently at university:

Dr Ovens' research, which was discussed last week at a conference at Nottingham Trent University titled Learning How to Learn in Higher Education, suggests that a growing proportion of students are 'puzzled' by the idea of independent learning.

This is because they have often been led through their schooling by their teachers, who he said were focused on 'meeting targets and Ofsted requirements'.

On his finding that one in three first-year undergraduates struggle to learn independently, he said: 'They are not taking control of their learning in the way we would want them to because they still want to be trained like they were at school.'

Dr Ovens added that the current generation of students had been assessed 'more than any other', and that the problem of dealing with students unused to independent learning was not unique to the UK: 'When we talk to colleagues worldwide, they have very similar problems, and they agree that the problems are getting progressively worse year on year.'

Current UK reforms focusing on the student experience carried the risk of a 'knee-jerk' response that would lead to even greater spoon-feeding of students, Dr Ovens said.

He argued that academics had to respond to these issues by treating students as independent scholars: 'Their autonomy is the single biggest value that can be developed; academics should not view students as empty vessels to be filled with knowledge.'[2]

So, the aim of many educationalists is to get pupils to practise using real-world problems. The aim of the RSA Opening Minds curriculum is as follows:

A competence based approach enables students not just to acquire subject knowledge but to understand, use and apply it within the context of their wider learning and life. It also offers students a more holistic and coherent way of learning which allows them to make connections and apply knowledge across different subject areas.[3]

The aim was to develop an approach which would ensure students were enabled to become responsible adults, active citizens, inquisitive lifelong learners and competent skilled employees.[4]

After all, so the argument runs, the important thing you take away from science lessons is not a body of scientific facts; it is the ability to think like a scientist. Likewise, the important thing you learn from history is not the list of dates. It is being able to think like an historian. The educationalist Anne de A'Echevarria puts it thus:

[Students] need to be adept in understanding how knowledge is formed within a particular discipline, how it changes and how they themselves may play a role in shaping, changing and working with such knowledge.

Enquiry pedagogy should be designed to help students uncover how a particular discipline generates that knowledge and understanding – to help students learn to think like historians, mathematicians, scientists or artists. Scientific content is a manifestation of scientific thinking, historical content is the manifestation of historical thinking, works of art are the manifestation of creative thinking. Students are disempowered if, in the main, they are required to internalise the products of other people's thinking, other people's questioning, other people's enquiries.[5]

So the theory is that to prepare pupils for the real world, we must introduce more real-world problems into the classroom. To get pupils to think like historians or scientists, we must introduce more tasks that involve them thinking like historians or scientists.

Modern practice

Sometimes this involves getting rid of subjects and teaching the entire curriculum through such integrated real-world problems. Sometimes it involves keeping subjects as an organising structure, but using more projects within them. It also involves giving pupils more independence and reducing the amount of teacher direction. We have seen examples of this already, in Chapter 2.

That is why in the RSA Opening Minds curriculum 'children plan their work, organise their own time and explore their own ways of learning'.[6] Ofsted are also particularly keen on this approach. They praise a number of lessons where even quite young pupils are given a great deal of autonomy and independence:

In a series of lessons on rivers, Year 4 pupils were given considerable control over their own learning. Guided by the teacher, they identified the key questions and decided how they might find and record the answers. They were also asked to decide how best to organise their time. In the first week, they decided that everyone would work on the same question. In the second week, they modified their approach so that different groups worked on different questions. They then evaluated both approaches and came to the conclusion that they were most effective when they all worked together on the same question. The teacher's records showed that this process had prompted some very mature thinking about how best to approach the process of learning.[7]

Year 4 pupils are also the subject of this RE lesson:

Pupils in Year 4 developed their own enquiries into key aspects of belief, based on key questions they framed in relation to the topic 'What do we believe?'[8]

Ofsted also encourage pupils to take on the role of teacher and assessor. In one subject report, they praise a lesson where pupils marked each other's work, singling out this comment as being particularly good:

> The following statement shows effective peer assessment by a student in his partner's geography exercise book. [The original phrasing, spelling and punctuation have been retained.]
> 'Tom I think you had a good range of facts and merged that with some explanations but you needed more to tell someone why it happened. The text is missing the journalists touch to it because it was if you remember, a newspaper article. Please make some arrangements to your spelling and use a wider range of vocabulary as you repeated some of your words. I would level this a level five slash six a. A picture possibly showing the volcano would be nice.'
> Signed E.[9]

One of Ofsted's most recent good practice resources for English is called Making English Real. It quotes a teacher as saying that the motivation for more realistic lessons is as follows:

> The English department aims to create and develop 'expert learners'. We are committed to establishing a learning environment that encourages students to feel confident about taking and acting on their own decisions. The primary focus will be on learning, rather than teaching, with students working in partnership with teachers, asking questions and reflecting on the learning strategies that work best for them.[10]

The lessons recommended in this report involve real-world problems that you might encounter in a job:

> The Year 7 unit on 'Improving the English department' aims to give students the opportunity to consider the best way to use an allocated amount of money in order to improve the department. As part of this work, students are expected to research and audit the resources currently available to teachers within the department and to conduct a survey to discover how teachers and learners would like to see the department improved. The work includes meetings of students in order to narrow the range of options, researching possible cross-curricular initiatives, and preparing proposals for the chosen projects that include costings and technical advice. Groups of students then present their ideas to the rest of the class.[11]

Another report praises similar realistic activities such as thinking about how to improve a part of the school, pitching ideas to others and sending emails:

> Students were invited to contribute to redesigning the school library to make it more eco-friendly. This was a highly effective start to the lesson and the students were very keen to help. It was explained that the task for students in the following week would be to 'pitch' their design ideas to the rest of the class using persuasive language and presentations involving information and communication technology. Students were put into pairs and asked to come up with one idea for 'greening' the library. They were later placed into one of four research groups to consider different environmental issues. Students acted as experts and moved to different groups to present the ideas from their first group. The lesson ended with some discussion of the linguistic features of emails as students were to compose email replies to the senior teacher outlining some of their initial ideas.[12]

Most of the English lessons discussed previously do not involve teaching literature. However, even when they do, Ofsted encourage a similar approach:

> These new units exist alongside more conventional topics, such as the study of classic texts including Shakespeare. However, the approach to these units is similar. For example, work on *Macbeth* involves students choosing scenes from the play to perform, making costumes, providing props, and, later, filming the outcome and presenting it to other students.[13]

The Association of Teachers and Lecturers praise one primary school's approach that focuses on teaching real-world problems and creating pupil experts:

> At Bealings Primary School the headteacher was inspired to revamp the curriculum and introduced REAL (Realistic Experience for Active Learning). Using extended role-play exercises, pupils are able to develop more realistic skills; the entire national curriculum is taught through this means. The curriculum is brought to life as pupils engage in fictional scenarios where they can act at being 'experts' working for a company.
>   Teachers continue with a project for as long as they feel the children are engaged and challenged. The children are able to build skills in teamwork, communication, independent learning and problem solving. Teachers at Bealings Primary believe that allowing the children to become 'experts' not only motivates them to learn but also dramatically changes the way they learn. Staff ensure that learning matches the national curriculum, however, the school feels that they have the freedom to teach it in a unique way. Children enjoy this way of learning and gain a better sense of reality, demonstrating confidence well beyond their years.[14]

In the theory section, we saw the educationalist Anne de A'Echevarria encourage teachers to get pupils to think like scientists. Here is the result of a practical activity that aimed to get pupils to think like designers (Figure 6.1).[15]

So the aim here is to give pupils complex, real-world tasks that will be more realistic, provide better motivation and help them become more adept at solving the kind of problems they will face outside the classroom. Pupils are also given very little guidance, as the aim is to ensure they can work independently.

Other types of projects involve practical activities that are linked to the content of the subject. In English, pupils engage in 'practical tasks such as making and using puppets as part of the *Romeo and Juliet* work'.[16] Similarly, in history, 'in the work on the British Empire, the students designed an Empire plate'.[17]

The following geography lesson involves pupils carrying out drama-based activities:

> Two pupils, in role, acted as newsreaders during an introductory simulation of a newscast. This used a PowerPoint backdrop and updated the rest of the class on the conflict. The teacher sat in the 'hot seat', acting as an expert to reflect on and clarify the issues. The pupils had a very good understanding of the differences between Hamas and Fatah and the tensions between Arabs and Israelis in the conflict. Having exemplified the role of

Figure 6.1 Think like designers activity: outcome of brainstorming session.

an 'expert witness', three pupils who had prepared scripts sat in 'hot seats'. Groups of pupils interviewed these experts – 'Is this an Arab/Israeli child?'; 'What are their concerns and worries?' and so on. This enabled pupils to develop a fresh perspective on the conflict and use their speaking, listening and questioning skills. They were able to explain the conflict through the eyes of children living within it today.[18]

A popular educational resources website is ActiveHistory (www.activehistory. co.uk). It is used by many schools in Britain and around the world, and many of them have written enthusiastic testimonials for it.[19] Its name gives a clue as to the type of resources it contains: they are all designed to promote the active learning of history, so nearly all of them involve pupils doing some kind of activity or project. The site contains hundreds of activities. One of the most popular is Design Your Own Heraldic Coat of Arms.[20] In this activity, the pupil has to select the best shape and colours to be used on their coat of arms. A screenshot from the activity is shown in Figure 6.2.

Another popular activity is the Black Death simulation. This is not just active, it is interactive. You pretend you are living in a medieval village and seeing the effects of the plague or Black Death.[21] You answer a series of questions like those in Figure 6.3.

You can see in the top left-hand corner of this activity that the pupils are given a mark for factual knowledge and sourcework skills. The factual knowledge consists of answering questions like the one shown in Figure 6.3.

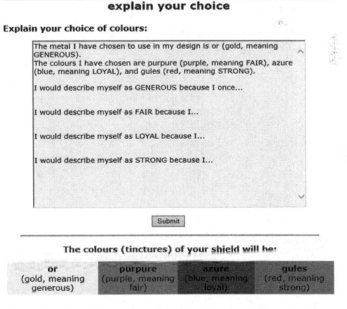

Figure 6.2 Screenshot from Design Your Own Heraldic Coat of Arms activity.

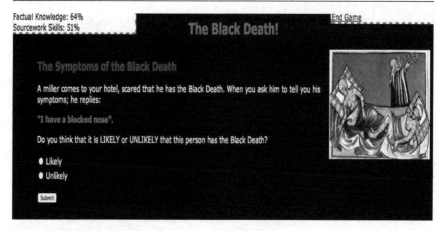

Figure 6.3 Question from the Black Death simulation.

So we can see here again that the knowledge pupils learn is co-constructed knowledge, not knowledge that is imposed on them by a teacher. By interacting with this computer simulation, they can construct the fact that a blocked nose was not a symptom of the Black Death.

We can see, therefore, that such projects and activities are popular in schools. They are seen as offering exciting real-world problems that will provide challenge and motivation and allow pupils to learn independently.

Why is this a myth?

First of all, let us address the idea that pupils should be taught to think like experts, or like scientists or historians. The difference between experts and novices is that experts have a huge body of background knowledge and processes stored in long-term memory, and that they have spent a huge amount of time practising using that knowledge and those processes. In most fields, it takes several years and thousands of hours to become an expert.[22] The knowledge and practice that experts have make a qualitative, not just a quantitative, difference to the way they think. The way they approach and solve problems is fundamentally different from the way novices approach problems. In the words of Dan Willingham, 'cognition early in training is fundamentally different from cognition late in training'.[23] There is no short-cut strategy or tactic that can bridge that gap.

Much of the practical evidence we have seen previously involves trying to make experts out of children who have not even been alive for ten years, let alone studying one field for that long. If you ask an expert to develop an enquiry into 'What do we believe?', their response will be informed by the knowledge they have about different belief systems and their functions. Year 4 pupils are eight or nine years old. The smartest, most intelligent and best-informed nine-year-old does not have that knowledge. Not only is it unrealistic to expect primary-age pupils to think like experts, it is unrealistic to expect school-leavers to think like experts. It is not a legitimate aim for primary or secondary general schooling. Not only that, but the types of tactics experts use to solve problems are not useful for novices who want to solve problems. One of the tactics experts use to great effect is to talk to themselves as they solve a problem.[24] It works for experts because of all the hidden background knowledge and processes they have. Recommending that pupils talk to themselves as they solve a problem would not have the effect of turning them into an expert. As we saw in Chapter 2, forcing pupils to be independent is not the best way to make them independent learners. Likewise, copying experts does not make you an expert. 'The practice of a profession is not the same as learning to practice the profession.'[25]

In short, copying what experts do does not make you an expert. An interesting analogy here is the famous cargo cult described by the theoretical physicist Richard Feynman:

> In the South Seas there is a cargo cult of people. During the war they saw airplanes with lots of good materials, and they want the same thing to happen now. So they've arranged to make things like runways, to put fires along the sides of the runways, to make a wooden hut for a man to sit in, with two wooden pieces on his head to headphones and bars of bamboo sticking out like antennas—he's the controller—and they wait for the airplanes to land. They're doing everything right. The form is perfect. It looks exactly the way it looked before. But it doesn't work. No airplanes land.[26]

At the root of this problem is a confusion of causation and correlation. The islanders realised that wearing coverings on your ears and gesturing towards the sky correlated with the delivery of cargo. They realised that there was some kind of a link between the two events. But they leapt from this point to assume that the former was the sole cause of the latter. They did not see – because they could not – all the other factors and events that went into the delivery of cargo. The soldiers who wore earphones and gestured at the sky were just a small and visible part of a highly complex process that was mostly invisible to the islanders. The visible parts of the process were important, of course. But they were only a small part of the process. By mimicking the visible, the islanders hoped to replicate the whole.

This seems to me the mistake we have made in encouraging expert performance among our pupils. We look at what experts do and encourage pupils to copy that. Remember the 'think like a designer' activity discussed earlier in this chapter (Figure 6.1), which encourages pupils to daydream in order to become good designers. This activity does not acknowledge the unseen knowledge and processes that allow expert designers to succeed. Top designers probably do daydream. So do poor designers, and so do people who cannot design at all. What separates an expert designer's daydreaming from a novice's daydreaming? It is the designer's specific knowledge and skills – and different types of designers will have very different types of knowledge and skills – which make such daydreaming profitable.

If it is unrealistic to expect school-leavers to be experts, however, it is clearly not unrealistic to expect them to be able to solve more simple real-world problems, such as how to make a room more environmentally friendly, or working out the best way you learn and adapting your activities accordingly. You do not have to be an expert to solve a real-world problem, and we all know adults who do have good problem-solving ability across a range of domains without being an expert in any of them. So the kernel of truth in this myth is that the aim of our teaching should be to equip pupils to be able to solve these problems, and to solve them independently. That is a legitimate and achievable aim. It is also true that real-world problems do not come neatly boxed in subject categories. But such independent problem-solving should be the final aim of education, not the sole method.

While you do not have to be an expert to solve a real-world problem, you still do need knowledge and practice. Take the project on greening the library, for example. This is indeed the sort of real-world project that an employee might be asked to do as part of their job. An educated adult employee is able to successfully tackle such a problem because they have certain bodies of knowledge and processes committed to memory. They know what a design pitch is; they know how to use information and communication technology effectively; they know certain facts about the environment; they know how to research; they know how to spell; they know how to write emails; and they know how to construct a sentence. They know all these things so well that it is easy for them to deploy the knowledge while solving the project. Pupils without that knowledge are not able to work successfully at the project. The amount of new information they meet will overload their working memory.

What this should also show us is that there is something deeply inequitable about the process of teaching projects. Such projects require background knowledge but they do nothing to teach it. Pupils who will do least badly at such projects are those who have gained background knowledge from elsewhere. As we have seen, the units of work on greening the library and *Macbeth* involved very little direct transmission of knowledge. They relied almost entirely on the knowledge about the environment and *Macbeth* that pupils brought to the lesson or that they could discover in the lesson. Clearly, pupils who had learned about the environment or *Macbeth* at home would have done a lot better in this project than pupils who had not. Those pupils will typically be advantaged pupils from wealthier backgrounds. This method is still not ideal for them – they would do better if they were taught facts at school as well as at home. But they will do better at such projects than their less advantaged peers, who will not have the background knowledge necessary to solve such problems and who do not have access to alternative means to make good their knowledge deficit.

This is one of the problems with the way we prepare pupils for examinations in England. It is true that English children are over-examined. It is often assumed that this means they must be overburdened with facts. The journalist Fran Abrams made this assumption repeatedly in a recent BBC radio programme about the English curriculum. In her words, 'there's been an increasing focus on knowledge, as English schools have become ever more exam-driven'.[27] However, this assumption is false. Just because our children are over-examined, it does not necessarily follow that they must therefore be overburdened with knowledge. It is a mistake to view English school-leaving examinations as being Gradgrindian tests of lists of facts. Most exams and coursework tasks actually involve pupils solving fairly real-world tasks, of the kind we have looked at. For example, most variations of the English GCSE exam involve the pupil reading an article from a real newspaper and answering some comprehension questions on it, then writing an email, an article or a speech that is again attuned to the real world. And of course, examinations are the ultimate independent task. There is not even minimal guidance allowed. I do not have a problem with this – after all, as I agreed at the start, we do need to make sure that at the end of our education system, pupils are able to solve real-world problems independently. As the exams I am talking about here do arrive at the end of the education system, then it is appropriate for them to ask pupils to solve real-world problems independently.

However, more and more schools are choosing to use final examination tasks to guide their curriculum in earlier years, and in many ways, the examination tasks have come to define the curriculum.[28] This is not entirely the fault of schools. They are under pressure to achieve exam results, and, as we have seen, the guidance on content that they used to receive from the National Curriculum has been withdrawn. If there is to be any point to a national curriculum, it is surely to do the kind of time-consuming and practical thinking about the type of knowledge you need to pass a final real-world exam task and the best way of sequencing that knowledge. In the absence of a curriculum doing this kind of heavy lifting, and in the presence of a powerful inspection agency that sees teaching as inimical to learning, it is understandable that schools have started to use past papers as the curriculum. The practical result of this is the same as the practical result of teaching projects. Pupils spend most of their time discussing how to answer exam and coursework tasks and actually answering exam and coursework tasks. They do not spend enough time being guided by the teacher to build up the hidden bodies of knowledge that actually allow you to succeed on such tasks. This is why students arrive at university unable to think independently. The counter-intuitive truth is that they are unable to think independently because they have always been taught as if they were already independent.

Something similar happens when projects are taught in younger years. As I made clear, the real-world project on greening the library is a serious one which might be attempted by a real employee. That is precisely why it is inappropriate for most pupils. In practice, it will result in confusion, frustration and demotivation. In practice, therefore, I think that most teachers end up altering the nature of these projects to make them more achievable. One approach is to alter the project so that it is less of a project – that is, to provide more structure and more guidance. I have taken this approach. For example, in a project that involved pupils writing any type of extended writing at the end, I would provide them with a help sheet summarising what they should put in each paragraph. This made the project more manageable, even as it made it less of a project. Yet it was not an effective strategy. Rather than breaking down the individual components required to write good reports and teaching those, I was asking pupils to write a report, and then giving them a few cheats or hints about how to do it. It is rather like teaching pupils a few cheats or hints that would help them learn how to play a certain song on the piano, while neglecting to teach them the scales and musical notation. These help sheets are not just my invention. You can find similar examples on Teachit (www.teachit.co.uk), a popular online library of English teaching resources.[29]

The other approach is to alter the project so that there is less of a focus on real-world tasks like extended writing, and more of a focus on other tasks that perhaps will not cause as much confusion. Again, this compromises the real-world aspect of the project, and it is also not particularly effective. This is also something I have done. I once taught a project on the history of football. I naively assumed that this would be a good project because the pupils were interested in football. But for it to have been worthwhile, the pupils would have needed some understanding of British history and British geography. They did not have this understanding. I did not want to spend time explaining about the Industrial Revolution and northern mill towns, because then it would not have been a project anymore and I would have been talking, which I knew was bad teaching practice.

I had planned that the pupils would do a piece of creative writing about what it was like to be a footballer in the nineteenth century and perhaps also some persuasive writing arguing for or against professionalism. This did not seem possible given how little they knew and how little I was allowed to tell them. The pupils ended up producing a portfolio of work from their lessons, one of the main items of which was their design for a football club's crest and a piece of written work evaluating its meaning. Lest this be seen as another example of anecdotal bad practice from me, let us look at the types of activities Ofsted and ActiveHistory recommend. Ofsted praise a history lesson where the pupils spend time designing an Empire plate and an English lesson where the pupils spend time making puppets. ActiveHistory recommends an activity very similar to mine – an activity where pupils design their own heraldic crest.

These types of activities are particularly wasteful because they involve pupils thinking about the wrong things. As we have seen, committing facts to long-term memory is vital. It is so vital that Kirschner and co-workers have gone so far as to say that 'the aim of all instruction is to alter long-term memory'.[30] Given this, then, it is very important that pupils remember as much as possible about what we want to teach them. Fortunately, the most effective way of remembering something is to think about it. The brain makes the assumption that anything it has to think about a lot must be important, so it is worthwhile committing it to long-term memory. In Dan Willingham's words, 'memory is the residue of thought'.[31] This makes sense, and it is also quite a nice insight because it means that if we spend a lot of class time getting pupils to think about what we want them to learn, we make it easier for them to commit such information to long-term memory.

So we need to make sure in our lessons and in the activities we plan that pupils think about the right things. One example of how not to do this is given by Dan Willingham. He says that in one history lesson about the Underground Railroad, a teacher got the pupils to bake cookies, because that was what slaves ate on the Underground Railroad.[32] For most of this lesson, the class will be thinking about the process of baking cookies — measuring the ingredients, turning on the oven, following the recipe. So this is a poor way to get them to learn about the Underground Railroad, as they will not actually spend most of the lesson thinking about it. Because of the importance of long-term memory, Willingham goes so far as to say that 'the most general and useful idea that cognitive psychology can offer teachers' is to 'review each lesson plan in terms of what the student is likely to think about'.[33]

Unfortunately, many of the activities described above fail this test. In the lesson I taught about the history of football, most of my pupils spent most of the time not thinking about history, or geography, or even football. They spent most of the time thinking about how to draw a crest shape and colouring in between the lines. Consider the English lesson on *Romeo and Juliet*, which involves making puppets. This involves pupils spending time thinking about the mechanics of puppet-making. That is not to say that colouring in and the mechanics of puppet-making are unimportant. The problem is that this lesson was an English lesson that was supposed to be about *Romeo and Juliet*. If the aim of the lesson was to teach pupils how to make a puppet, it would have been a good lesson.

Not only do these types of activities fail in their ultimate aims, but because they are so time-consuming they also have a very significant opportunity cost. Many year 9 pupils have only one or two hours of history a week. If they have two hours per week and spend two hours per half term doing something like designing an Empire plate, or answering a series of questions about their personality and using the answers to design a coat of arms, then for one-sixth of the time when they are meant to be studying history, they are not really thinking about history.

One irony to note is that these types of lessons are often presented as imaginative alternatives to dull rote learning. However, given what we know about how we remember things, it is paradoxically this kind of lesson plan and unit of work that does lead to dull rote learning. In the Shakespeare puppet lesson, the pupils will have spent several lessons where they have not actually thought about Shakespeare or *Romeo and Juliet*. The important knowledge and skills that they should have been thinking about and practising will be hurried and squeezed into just a few lessons, probably in quite a mechanistic way. If there is an assessment on this unit, then because there has not been enough time in the lessons to think about these facts in a meaningful way, the only solution for the pupil who wants to revise is to rote learn them – that is, to learn the facts in a way that is stripped of meaning. If you waste class time on tangential and distracting activities, then pupils will end up rote learning – and probably rote mislearning – the important knowledge and skills that they should have been taught meaningfully.

In Chapter 2 we looked at the success of direct instruction. We can see now exactly why it is so superior to alternative, minimally guided approaches, such as projects and activities. In that chapter, I looked at why direct instruction and drill were such effective methods for Winston Churchill, who was not a particularly bright pupil. Now, I would like to show why an artificial, drill-based approach is more effective for very talented pupils too.

In football, you eventually want a football team to play an 11-a-side game and win that game. But the best way to achieve that is *not* to get children playing regular competitive 11-a-side games from a young age. Just as with projects, you should break down the complex problem of winning an 11-a-side game into smaller, simpler problems, and practise those. The fundamental basic team skill required in football is to be able to keep the ball. The fundamental basic individual skill follows from this – it is to be able to control the ball, which means having a good first touch, and being able to give and take a pass. Churchill realised that the important fundamental building block of the English language is the sentence. He realised how valuable it was to 'get into his bones' the structure of the English sentence.[34] If you cannot construct a sentence, you cannot write. If you cannot control a football, you cannot play football.

As I have shown, getting pupils to do lots and lots of complex tasks often makes it harder for them to achieve mastery of the important elements that make up complex tasks. Instead, it may actually lead to them forgetting them or neglecting them. Similarly, playing 11-a-side football games between 11-year-olds on full-sized pitches will almost certainly not lead to those children mastering the ability to pass and control the ball. In England, however, that is how we teach children to play football. In the under-11 age group, they essentially play the same game that adults do on the same sized pitches.[35] In the terms I have been using, children are encouraged to attempt a complex real-world task at an early age. In Spain and Latin America, children focus much,

much more on ball skills and drills. These are entirely artificial and decontextualised. They will not involve trying to score a goal; they often involve cones marking out a very small space, and often there will not be any opposition players or any tackling. A lot of the time, children will play *futsal*, a five-a-side indoor game with small goals and no offside rule; the game was created in Uruguay in the early 1930s.[36]

Even when they do start to play outdoor games, they remain small-sided. In Spain, children do not play 11-a-side games on full-sized pitches until they reach the under-14 age group.[37] The point of all these drills, artificial rules and small games is for the young footballers to master the skills that truly matter for the adult game. The Spanish system has realised that you do not have to endlessly play the adult game to develop expertise at it; in fact, endlessly playing 11-a-side games on full-sized pitches may not actually develop your expertise. To improve as a footballer, you need to touch the ball. When 11-year-olds play 11-a-side games, they do not touch the ball as much as if they are playing smaller-sided games and lots of players will barely touch the ball at all. And it works: the players who make up the world's most successful club and national 11-a-side teams did not start playing 11-a-side games until three years later than their less successful English counterparts. They will have had much less experience of real-world games. But they will have had much more experience of what matters in a real-world game: controlling the ball.

Exactly the same problem affects the teaching of English. In so very many of the lessons and projects I have discussed, pupils are expected to finish the project by doing a piece of extended writing – either a report, or an email, or a letter, or a piece of persuasive writing. This is seen as sufficient for the teaching of English. But actually, in most of these projects, the pupils have not been taught to write at all. They have been asked to do some writing, which is not at all the same thing. Grammatical knowledge, which is one of the most fundamental bodies of knowledge you need to be able to write well, is barely taught. In the 34 English lessons described in the two most recent Ofsted English subject reports, only one involves any mention of grammar:

> For example, younger students especially enjoy the 'Mr Men' unit of work. While this might seem on the surface to make limited demands on the ability of secondary-age students, the work involves a great deal of grammatical and linguistic analysis. The unit begins with an exploration of the notion of stereotypes. Students then review and extend their knowledge of grammar focusing on the use of adjectives, onomatopoeia and alliteration. This leads into an analysis of Mr Men characters, analysing the author's use of these techniques before students create their own new character.[38]

Unfortunately, onomatopoeia and alliteration are not actually examples of grammatical features. They are stylistic devices. So, the only grammar lesson Ofsted praise is not actually a grammar lesson. The Ofsted inspectors' confusion about grammar is not unusual. In the decades after the 1960s, grammar teaching fell out of fashion in English schools.[39] Although some of the earlier iterations of the English NC tried to reintroduce it, this curriculum had to be delivered by teachers who had not themselves been taught about grammar. Surveys in 1995 and 2002 showed that trainee teachers had significant gaps in their grammatical knowledge that were not being addressed.[40] So, while there may have been some official publications about the importance of grammar in the 1990s, in terms of actual classroom practice we have still not managed to overcome the knowledge deficit brought about by the decline of grammar teaching in the 1960s. Ofsted's reports, which mention grammar only to get it wrong, clearly show this.

Perhaps it is because teachers and Ofsted inspectors are uncertain about the type of grammatical knowledge they should teach that they are so wary of teaching it. Whatever the cause, the result is that Ofsted encourage a cargo cult approach, which involves pupils copying what real writers do instead of taking the time to learn and practise the fundamental knowledge that real writers have. In both the English school system and the football system, it is possible to muddle through without your weakness at the basics ever being properly identified and corrected. The English Football Association have recognised this problem and are trying to reorganise youth football so that players get more of a chance to practise the basics. The English education authorities, however, have shown no such willingness to change.

Like so many of the myths we have encountered, this one has noble aims and dreadful methods. The aim of education should be for our pupils to be able to solve real-world problems on their own. But we will not achieve that aim if we begin by teaching them as though they can already solve real-world problems on their own.

Notes

1   Wheeler, S. Content as curriculum (2012), http://steve-wheeler.blogspot. co.uk/2011/12/content-as-curriculum.html (accessed 6 March 2013).
2   *Times Higher Education Supplement.* To spoon-feed is not to nurture (2011), www. timeshighereducation.co.uk/story.asp?storycode=418217 (accessed 6 March 2013).
3   Royal Society of Arts Opening Minds. Opening Minds (2013), www.thersa.org/ action-research-centre/education/practical-projects/opening-minds (accessed 7 March 2013).
4   Royal Society of Arts Opening Minds. Why was RSA Opening Minds developed? (2013), www.rsaopeningminds.org.uk/about-rsa-openingminds/why-was-opening-minds-developed/ (accessed 6 March 2013).
5   de A'Echevarria, A. Exploring subject-specific enquiry skills (2008), www.teaching expertise.com/e-bulletins/subjects-specific-thinking-skills-3837 (accessed 6 March 2013).

6   Royal Society of Arts Opening Minds. RSA Opening Minds competence framework   (2013),   www.rsaopeningminds.org.uk/about-rsa-openingminds/ competences/ (accessed 6 March 2013).

7   Office for Standards in Education, Children's Services and Skills. Curriculum innovation in schools (2008), p. 13, www.ofsted.gov.uk/resources/curriculum-innovation-schools (accessed 6 March 2013).

8   Office for Standards in Education, Children's Services and Skills. Transforming religious education: Religious education in schools 2006–09 (2010), p. 27, www. ofsted.gov.uk/resources/transforming-religious-education (accessed 6 March 2013).

9   Office for Standards in Education, Children's Services and Skills. Geography: Learning to make a world of difference (2011), p. 30, www.ofsted.gov.uk/ resources/geography-learning-make-world-of-difference (accessed 6 March 2013).

10 Office for Standards in Education, Children's Services and Skills. Good practice resource: Making English real – creating independent learners in English: The Peele Community College October (2011), p. 2, www.ofsted.gov.uk/resources/good-practice-resource-making-english-real-creating-independent-learners-english-peele-community-col (accessed 6 March 2013).

11 Ibid., pp. 2–3.

12 Office for Standards in Education, Children's Services and Skills. Excellence in English: What we can learn from 12 outstanding schools (2011), pp. 27–28, www. ofsted.gov.uk/resources/excellence-english (accessed 6 March 2013).

13 Office for Standards in Education, Children's Services and Skills. Good practice resource: Making English real – creating independent learners in English: The Peele Community College October (2011), p. 3, www.ofsted.gov.uk/resources/ good-practice-resource-making-english-real-creating-independent-learners-english-peele-community-col (accessed 6 March 2013).

14 Association of Teachers and Lecturers. Subject to change: new thinking on the curriculum (2007), p. 35, www.atl.org.uk/Images/Subject%20to%20change.pdf (accessed 6 March 2013).

15 de A'Echevarria, A. Y10 model of the creative process (2008), www. teachingexpertise.com/files/Y10 model of the creative process.pdf (accessed 6 March 2013).

16 Office for Standards in Education, Children's Services and Skills. Moving English forward: Action to raise standards in English (2012), pp. 32–33, www.ofsted.gov. uk/resources/moving-english-forward (accessed 6 March 2013).

17 Office for Standards in Education, Children's Services and Skills. History for all: History in English schools 2007/10 (2011), p. 14, www.ofsted.gov.uk/resources/ history-for-all (accessed 6 March 2013).

18 Office for Standards in Education, Children's Services and Skills. Geography: Learning to make a world of difference (2011), p. 36, www.ofsted.gov.uk/ resources/geography-learning-make-world-of-difference (accessed 6 March 2013).

19 ActiveHistory.co.uk. Testimonies (2013), www.activehistory.co.uk/testimonies. htm (accessed 6 March 2013).

20 ActiveHistory.co.uk. Design Your Own Coat of Arms (2013), www.activehistory. co.uk/main_area/games/yr7_heraldry/frameset.htm (accessed 6 March 2013).

21 ActiveHistory.co.uk (2013). The Black Death, www.activehistory.co.uk/ Miscellaneous/menus/Year_7/Black_Death.htm (accessed 7 March 2013).

22 Simon, H. and Chase, W. Skill in chess. *American Scientist* 1973; 61: 394–403; Ericsson, K.A., Krampe, R.T. and Tesch-Römer, C. The role of deliberate practice in the acquisition of expert performance. *Psychological Review* 1993; 100: 363–406; Ericsson, K.A., Charness, N., Hoffman, R.R. and Feltovich, P.J. *The Cambridge Handbook of Expertise and Expert Performance.* New York: Cambridge University Press, 2006.

23 Willingham, D.T. *Why Don't Students Like School?* San Francisco: Jossey-Bass, 2009, p. 127.

24 Ibid., p. 137.

25 Kirschner, P.A., Sweller, J. and Clark, R.E. Why minimal guidance during instruction does not work: an analysis of the failure of constructivist, discovery, problem-based, experiential, and inquiry-based teaching. *Educational Psychologist* 2006; 41: 75–86.

26 Feynman, R. *'Surely You're Joking, Mr Feynman?'* London: Vintage, 1992, p. 340.

27 BBC Radio Four Current Affairs. School of hard facts: transcript of a recorded documentary (originally broadcast on 22 October 2012) (2012), http://news.bbc.co.uk/1/shared/spl/hi/programmes/analysis/transcripts/221012.pdf (accessed 6 March 2013).

28 Department for Education. Early entry to GCSE examinations (2011), p. 3, www.education.gov.uk/publications/eOrderingDownload/DFE-RR208.pdf (accessed 7 March 2013); Oates, T. Could do better: Using international comparisons to refine the National Curriculum in England (2010), p. 7,www.cambridgeassessment.org.uk/ca/digitalAssets/188853_Could_do_better_FINAL_inc_foreword.pdf (accessed 7 March 2013).

29 *The Signal-Man* by Charles Dickens (2013), p. 6, www.teachit.co.uk/attachments/1573.pdf (accessed 6 March 2013); The duality of *Dr Jekyll and Mr Hyde* (2005), p. 2, www.teachit.co.uk/attachments/4001.pdf (accessed 6 March 2013).

30 Kirschner, P.A., Sweller, J. and Clark, R.E. Why minimal guidance during instruction does not work: An analysis of the failure of constructivist, discovery, problem-based, experiential, and inquiry-based teaching. *Educational Psychologist* 2006; 41: 75–86.

31 Willingham, D.T. *Why Don't Students Like School?* San Francisco: Jossey-Bass, 2009, p. 54.

32 Ibid., p. 53.

33 Ibid., p. 79.

34 Churchill, W. *A Roving Commission: My Early Life.* New York: C. Scribner's Sons, 1939, p. 16.

35 *Guardian.* FA votes for smaller-sided matches for young footballers (2012), www.guardian.co.uk/football/2012/may/28/fa (accessed 6 March 2013).

36 The FA com. The history of futsal (2013), www.thefa.com/my-football/player/futsal/history-of-futsal (accessed 6 March 2013).

37 BBC Sport Football. Gareth Southgate reveals FA youth football initiative (2011), www.bbc.co.uk/sport/0/football/13634800 (accessed 6 March 2013).

38 Office for Standards in Education, Children's Services and Skills. Excellence in English: What we can learn from 12 outstanding schools (2011), p. 27, www.education.gov.uk/publications/eOrderingDownload/100229.pdf (accessed 3 March 2013).

39 Hudson, R. and Walmsley, J. The English patient: English grammar and teaching in the twentieth century. *Journal of Linguistics* 2005; 41: 593–622.
40 See: Williamson, J. and Hardman, F. Time for refilling the bath? A study of primary student-teachers' grammatical knowledge. *Language and Education* 1995; 9: 117–134; Cajkler, W. and Hislam, J. Trainee teachers' grammatical knowledge: The tension between public expectations and individual competence. *Language Awareness* 2002; 11: 161–177.

Myth 7

Teaching knowledge is indoctrination

Where is the evidence that people believe this and that it has affected education policy and classroom practice?

Theoretical evidence

One frequent criticism of knowledge-based curricula is that selecting the knowledge on the curriculum is inevitably a politically biased act which risks indoctrinating pupils with the values of those doing the selecting.

The theory here is that knowledge is a tricky concept. It is all very well to say that you want to teach children knowledge, but this brings a host of problems in its wake. We might agree on the existence of certain objective facts, but there are lots of them. How are we to decide which facts to teach? What criteria should we use to decide what gets to be taught and what does not?

In the 1960s and 1970s, some theorists even suggested that it was hard to agree even on the existence of certain objective facts. In *The Social Construction of Reality: A Treatise in the Sociology of Knowledge*, published in 1966, Berger and Luckmann looked at the way that many of the facts we perceived to be true were in fact social constructions.[1] They did not objectively exist *out there* somewhere. They were brought into being because we all believed in them, and very often they were buttressed by institutional power.

Educationalists applied this theory to the curriculum. If the 'facts' we take for granted are just constructions of society, then how can we base a curriculum on them? Not only that, but if the 'facts' are constructed by our social systems and institutions, then education becomes implicit in their establishment and preservation. Traditional curricula privilege certain types of knowledge, but there is no objective justification for that; it is just a social construction and convention. If we follow this argument, then teaching facts, or teaching knowledge, stops being the neutral activity it seemed up until then. Instead it becomes intimately bound up with questions of power, authority and social class. Many of the educationalists pioneering this thought were based at the Institute of Education in London, and many of them feature in a collection of essays edited by Michael Young in 1971, *Knowledge and Control: New Directions for the Sociology of Education*.[2] Young himself wrote the following:

> those in positions of power will attempt to define what is to be taken as knowledge, how accessible to different groups any knowledge is, and what are the accepted relationships between different knowledge areas and between those who have access to them and make them available.[3]

The theorists in this collection were of course writing in the days before the National Curriculum (NC). The kind of school knowledge they were attacking here was not, therefore, the type mandated by law by the NC. They were attacking society's hegemonic values, which are not only found in statute, but also in the 'constitutive principles, codes, and especially the commonsense consciousness and practices underlying our lives'.[4] Thus, even before the creation of the NC, they attacked the way that certain subjects and types of knowledge were imposed on children, the imposition being done not by law but by our socially constructed understanding that certain types of knowledge were better than others. For Vic Kelly, such imposition was undemocratic: 'one must see the imposition of any one version of knowledge as a form of social control and as a threat to all of the major freedoms identified as essential constituents of a free and democratic society.'[5] He also noted that 'postmodernism … undermines any theories anyone might mount for the God-given right of any body of "knowledge", school subject or whatever to be included in a compulsory curriculum'.[6]

Another frequent concern of these theorists is the nature of social class and the curriculum. Geoff Whitty explained that when he first began teaching a 'grammar school curriculum' to a class of working-class comprehensive pupils, the experience was meaningless to them.[7] John White explored how our current curriculum subjects are a 'traditional middle-class curriculum' and how imposing them on everyone 'privileges the middle class'.[8] The Association of Teachers and Lecturers' (ATL) report on the curriculum argues that 'high culture is closely related to the lifestyle of an upper class' and criticises the way that twentieth-century education tried to teach high culture to the masses: 'mass education systems developed in the twentieth century copied the curriculum considered necessary for social elites'.[9] It can be seen from this that these theorists are particularly concerned with the experience of working-class, disadvantaged and underprivileged children. They want to secure a curriculum that is democratic and egalitarian, one that is designed to help every child learn and not just to reproduce the interests of the dominant class.

Attitudes to the NC among such theorists are mixed. To begin with, they were mostly fiercely critical of it, seeing it as an attempt to shore up the hegemony of traditional subjects and knowledge. Over time, their attitudes softened, particularly after the 1999 and 2007 curriculum revisions. Martin Johnson praised the 2007 reforms as 'a step in the direction we propose', although he queried if it would be a big enough step.[10] John White served on the 2007 reform committee, and was pleased with both the 1999 and 2007 lists of curriculum aims.[11]

Who are the people I have just quoted? Martin Johnson, the General Secretary of the ATL, we have met before. He is the main author of the ATL's 2007 curriculum report, *Subject to Change*. Michael Young, Michael Apple, Geoff Whitty, Vic Kelly and John White are all influential curriculum theorists. Michael Young, interestingly, has altered his views in a quite significant way over the past decade. Michael Apple is American, but his work has been fairly influential in the academy here: *Ideology and Curriculum* was first published in 1979 and is now in its third edition.[12] Between 2000 and 2010, Geoff Whitty was the Director of the Institute of Education, one of the most influential and prestigious educational institutions in the UK. Vic Kelly died in 2010, but before that he was Emeritus Professor at Goldsmiths and before that the Dean of Education there. His text *The Curriculum: Theory and Practice* was first published in 1977 and it is now in its sixth edition, which was published in 2009. It is featured on many university education departments' reading lists, and its blurb features a quotation from a current Institute of Education senior lecturer, who lauds it as a 'curriculum classic'.[13] John White is an Emeritus Professor at the Institute of Education and advised on the 2007 curriculum reforms.[14] I mention all this just to show that I am not attacking straw men. These theorists are real people who have had significant direct and indirect influence over school education over the past 40 years.

What we can see is that for all of them, the very concept of knowledge is problematic. Knowledge is bound up with issues of social class and power. There is no one absolute right body of knowledge we can teach. To try to teach one risks indoctrinating pupils. The traditional curriculum and the NC involve teaching knowledge that reproduces hegemonic values and therefore reproduces social and class inequalities. What is the poor teacher to do? The solution is either not to teach knowledge, or to refocus classroom practice away from knowledge and towards skills. As Vic Kelly said, education should be about giving pupils 'the right to negotiate meanings, to interpret and reinterpret their own experiences and thus, crucially, to develop their own systems of values'.[15] John White wanted government to 'positively encourage schools to diverge from traditional approaches' of organising the curriculum, and to move towards 'projects, interdisciplinary activities or other ways not based on discrete subjects'.[16] In another article, he asks 'why is knowledge acquisition what schools should be about? Some people would say they should also be about developing the imagination, wider sympathies with other people, a love of beauty, personal qualities like confidence'[17] So, the theory tells us that we should not impose external content on pupils but instead work with the knowledge and experiences they already have to develop their abilities, preferably through projects that are not as middle-class as traditional subjects.

Modern practice

We have seen already that attitudes to the 1999 and 2007 curriculum revisions were mixed. But in practice, it is fair to say that these revisions took on board many of the theoretical criticisms of the curriculum. These revisions both reduced the amount of content on the curriculum and placed more of an emphasis on the skills pupils should develop. The 2007 curriculum particularly encouraged teachers to think of lessons more as a series of learning experiences, where pupils could negotiate the meanings of the knowledge that they brought to the classroom.

We have also seen that the lessons recommended by Ofsted fit in with this practice. There are plenty of lessons where there is limited subject content. In place of this, pupils are encouraged to spend time creating their own content, which is then used as a subject for study by others, as in this English lesson:

> A year 9 lesson had objectives related to 'working considerately' as a group and providing positive and constructive feedback on each other's work. The teacher highlighted these points and gave examples of effective feedback just before the class watched a group of students presenting their own television documentary. He modelled the process by taking notes during the presentation. Spontaneous applause followed the group presentation, and students gave positive comments and some sensitively expressed criticism.[18]

The same is true of this art lesson:

> Students had been thinking about the lesson in advance. They arrived with an artefact of personal significance that remained a mystery to the teacher or other students at the start of the lesson. Their attention was immediately attracted to a large cardboard box sitting in the middle of the classroom. Small movements and strange sounds emerging from the box promoted intense curiosity.
>
> The students were quick to accept the teachers' challenge to record their ideas and feelings, using paper and drawing tools arranged around the box. Observing a tendency to draw animals that might sit inside the box, the teacher demanded that they push their imagination to the limits; 'If there is a creature inside, how frantic is it? Are your drawings frantic? If it is dark and scary inside, how dark and scary are your drawings?' Encouraged to use words, the students explored how to represent 'trapped', 'intimidated', 'cornered', by gesturing more through their drawing. Lively, expressive drawings emerged showing layers of meaning. Ten minutes into the lesson the depth of students' thinking, and fluency in the use of drawing, had progressed significantly.

Continuing with minimal teacher talk, the students returned to their chosen objects, reflecting on and explaining their significance. Listening carefully, the teacher again used minimal questioning to promote deeper analysis. Building on their experience of drawing from imagination, the teacher encouraged the students to use drawing to represent the meaning of their object, getting 'into the mindset of an artist'. The teacher challenged the students further, by asking them to reflect on what the drawings revealed about the significance of objects chosen by other students. Moving speedily from drawing to drawing every student was expected to add further emphasis to the meaning. Returning to drawings of their own object, now enriched by drawing additions by other students, the teacher linked the activity to that of an artist seeing their work in a gallery evaluated by others, through the experience every individual brings. Half an hour into the lesson the teacher shared the objective; 'To increase understanding about purpose and meaning in artists' work.'[19]

Or, pupils work with the knowledge they already bring to the classroom, as in this RE lesson:

At the end, the students were asked to write an account of reality from their own perspective. They engaged enthusiastically with what they saw as a challenging task. Some offered a view which reflected their own sense of living in a diverse world, where people no longer believe in certainties.[20]

Or, pupils work with knowledge that might be considered to be more relevant to them, as in this English lesson:

Another key feature in the department's success is that students, as well as all staff, contribute directly to planning schemes of work in English. Topics and approaches are proposed and evaluated through discussion in lessons and through consultation with students representing the range of ability and aspiration. The curriculum has also been constructed so that there are clear, shared priorities that directly address local and community needs, such as:

- to explore themes relevant to students' experience, for example, looking at how media target and manipulate children
- to reflect the school's growing diversity and tackle south-east London issues such as refugees, racism, and street culture.[21]

Here is another example, also from an English lesson:

The class with less able students worked together, looking first at a Gary Lineker webpage, then at a news item about his impending divorce.[22]

On the rare occasions when they do encounter new knowledge that they have not created, the emphasis is always on making such content relevant to pupils:

> Another Year 9 lesson explored the relationship between Pip's adoptive parents in Great Expectations. The teacher's plan included family relationships and resolution of family issues. Students chose to explore these ideas by role-playing marriage guidance sessions and hot-seating different characters. In the work and plenary which followed, students displayed unusual seriousness and trust in each other as they explored complex issues including family abuse. In this way, the study of texts was constantly related to contemporary life and students' own experiences.[23]

Of the 33 English lessons or curriculum units summarised in the most recent two Ofsted English reports, 19 involve no mention of any literary or grammatical content.[24] Even in the 14 lessons that do mention such content, the content is very often not the focus of the lesson. For example, there is the lesson on *Romeo and Juliet*, where the pupils make puppets; the lesson on *Great Expectations*, where the focus is on role-playing marriage guidance sessions; the lesson on Shakespeare's plays, where the stress is on film-making; and the lesson on *Macbeth*, which is praised not because of anything in the lesson, but because pupils emailed their homework on it to the teacher. Even in these 14 cases where literary or grammatical content is mentioned, only a limited proportion of the time involves teachers teaching the content and pupils thinking about it; much more time is spent on pupil-led activities designed to try to make the new knowledge relevant to their lives.

Why is this a myth?

I would agree completely with these theorists' concern for democracy and equality. When John White says that curriculum planning should start 'with a picture ... of what it is to lead a flourishing personal and civic life in a modern liberal democracy', I could not agree more.[25] Where our society is democratic and equal, education should aim to help preserve that situation; where it is not, education should seek to change it. It is because I agree with the aims of these theorists that I so profoundly disagree with their methods. To reduce and marginalise the teaching of knowledge in schools will increase the undemocratic and unequal features of our society.

As we have seen, it is not possible to separate skills and knowledge in the easy way some of these theorists consider. John White wanted schools to focus on 'developing the imagination, wider sympathies with other people, a love of beauty, personal qualities like confidence' rather than the acquisition of knowledge, but as we have seen, these skills and abilities are not as separable from the acquisition of knowledge as he assumes.[26] If it were possible to teach skills in the abstract without recourse to knowledge, then this might be a solution. But it is not. In practice, we know this is the case because all of the Ofsted lesson descriptions we have seen do have to include knowledge of some kind. It is just that, as we have also seen, it is often the type of knowledge pupils know already. Again, were skill transferability as easy as these theorists suppose, this might be an option. But it is not. If pupils learn how to understand the political dynamics of their class relationships, that does not mean they can then understand a historical article about the political dynamics of the Long Parliament.

It might still be argued, however, that knowledge of the political dynamics of the Long Parliament is irrelevant. Why should a pupil need to know anything external to them which they cannot themselves experience? And who is to say that knowledge of the things external to them is somehow better, or more valid, than knowledge of your own circumstances? I would argue that if you really are concerned with democracy and equality, such knowledge is vital. Democracy requires every citizen to have knowledge and understanding of the world beyond their immediate experience; equality requires that there should be no great gaps in this understanding between people or social classes. To be an active citizen of a democratic society you have to know about history, the world, science, the arts. You have to know about things that most pupils do not bring to the classroom and which they cannot pick up through experience. The socialist historian R.H. Tawney made this point:

> No one can be fully at home in the world unless, through some acquaintance with literature and art, the history of society and the revelations of science, he has seen enough of the triumphs and tragedies of mankind to realise the heights to which human nature can rise and the depths to which it can sink.[27]

Knowledge of the external world is also important for equality. If you only teach pupils using the knowledge they bring to the classroom and the knowledge they might pick up through experience, then you will reproduce educational inequalities. Pupils from educated families will bring a great deal of knowledge to the classroom. Pupils from uneducated and immigrant families will bring less knowledge.

William Beveridge recognised the importance of knowledge for a democracy. Ignorance was one of his five social evils; he also said 'ignorance is an evil weed, which dictators may cultivate among their dupes, but which no democracy can afford among its citizens'.[28] Thomas Jefferson too recognised how knowledge matters for freedom: 'If a nation expects to be ignorant and free in a state of civilisation, it expects what never was and never will be.'[29]

In practice, I have found this to be very true. I have taught many sixth-formers who had received top grades throughout their education but who lacked the background knowledge necessary to make the kind of informed decisions we require of our citizens. Once, in a discussion about elections and democracy, a sixth-former asked me if you could vote for the Queen. Many of the students I have taught have been uncertain about who or what you get to vote for in elections. The Hansard Society's yearly audit of political engagement suggests that my experiences are not unique: in their survey, only a third of 18–24-year-olds got more than 66 per cent correct answers on a simple true-or-false quiz about British politics.[30] The survey does not provide question-by-question breakdowns for each age category. However, one-third of all age groups answered 'true' to the following statement: Members of the House of Lords are elected by the British public.[31] As ever, this should remind us of how fundamental knowledge is for all higher-order thinking. Quite clearly, people who think that members of the House of Lords are elected are not going to be able to analyse and evaluate all the topical arguments for and against reform of the Lords. They are lacking crucial knowledge about the House of Lords, and that knowledge can not be adequately supplied by generic 'questioning' skills. I think it is also true that if your knowledge of our democratic institutions is this uncertain, people will find it much easier to manipulate and mislead you. As Beveridge noted, bias stems from ignorance, not from knowledge. The best defence against bias is not questioning. The best defence is knowledge. If you do not know the facts, you will not know if there is anything that needs questioning.

We can therefore see the value of teaching external knowledge in the classroom. But this still does not solve the problem of what knowledge and whose knowledge. How do we make sure that knowledge is not inherently biased or subjective or representative only of a small elite? Is there any way of doing this? Dan Willingham offers one suggestion. Rather than making value judgements about what knowledge is more important or more deserving of inclusion into a curriculum, we can instead ask: 'What knowledge yields the greatest cognitive benefit?'[32] For the specific but very important case of reading, we have seen that the knowledge that yields the greatest cognitive benefit is the type of knowledge that is taken for granted by writers. This is the kind of knowledge that pupils have to have to make inferences. If our aim is for our pupils to read broadsheet newspapers and intelligent books aimed at a non-specialist audience, then we should teach the kind of knowledge these writers assume their readers have. As Willingham notes:

> Using that criteria, we may still be distressed that much of what writers assume their readers know seems to be touchstones of the culture of dead white males. From the cognitive scientist's point of view, the only choice in that case is to try to persuade writers and editors at the Washington Post, Chicago Tribune, and so on to assume different knowledge on the part of their readers.[33]

Willingham is right to note 'that much of what writers assume their readers know seems to be touchstones of the culture of dead white males'. In the

United States, empirical analyses of newspaper texts bear this out.[34] They also show that such knowledge is much less transient than we think: while it shifts around the edges, the core remains stable. Hirsch used these analyses (as well as input from teachers and academics) to create the Core Knowledge curriculum. It has since been adopted by 768 US schools and its principles informed the successful reform of the curriculum in Massachusetts in 1993.[35]

No such similar analysis of the knowledge writers take for granted has been done in Britain. A British corpus of this kind would undoubtedly be different, and it is to be hoped that a British scholar will undertake something like this soon. In the meantime, the American corpus, the relatively traditional knowledge it contains and the logic behind it mean that we know enough to be able to make a good approximation of the kind of knowledge British writers take for granted.

As Willingham suggests, we might be depressed at the pre-eminence of dead white men, but we might also consider the reasons for this. Shakespeare's plays, characters and language have proved remarkably enduring and knowledge of them is useful in cognitive terms for people learning to read any nation's version of English. It could be argued that their success is merely the result of Western hegemonic power. But it could also be argued that it is because ordinary people around the world have found in his plays a unique and timeless insight into the human condition. After all, Maya Angelou said that when she first read Shakespeare, she was convinced he was a black woman.[36] Nelson Mandela read his words on courage and cowardice while imprisoned on Robben Island.[37] Marcel Reich-Ranicki, a survivor of the Warsaw Ghetto, has related how Shakespeare's words were relevant to him at the most desperate time in his life.[38]

If we still, however, feel that the pre-eminence of the culture of dead white Western men is unmerited and merely a function of their economic and military power, then we *still* need to teach them. If we do not teach that knowledge, the outcome will not be that the wider culture realises that the status of the dead white Western culture is unmerited. We will just ensure that our pupils have no knowledge of that culture, which will exclude them from the ability to contribute to debates about it, and from many other important debates as well. As Willingham notes, 'without that knowledge, [students] cannot read the breadth of material that their more knowledgeable schoolmates can, nor with the depth of comprehension'.[39]

That is an approach that can help us decide on the breadth of knowledge we should teach across the curriculum to help reading. That is because reading requires broad knowledge, but such knowledge does not have to be that deep. To develop skills other than reading, pupils need deep knowledge of certain concepts. Which concepts should these be? 'Cognitive science leads to the rather obvious conclusion that students must learn the concepts that come up again and again – the unifying ideas of each discipline.'[40] How should we decide which disciplines we teach and which concepts are the fundamental

ones? This is another topic that has been a hugely controversial. For many of
the theorists we looked at, subject disciplines were themselves artificial
inventions designed to enforce Victorian middle-class values. Is this the case? If
so, it is odd to think that a range of very diverse countries and cultures have
ended up using very similar school subjects to the ones deemed to be Victorian
and middle-class.[41] Rather than assuming that countries as diverse as Finland
and South Korea spontaneously decided to take the Victorian middle-class
school curriculum as their model, I think a more plausible explanation is that
subjects are very useful. They may well be human inventions, but they are very
useful human inventions because they provide a practical way of teaching the
kinds of important concepts Willingham talks about. The sentence in English,
place value in mathematics, energy in physics: in each case, subjects provide a
useful framework for teaching the concept. And in each case, the concept is a
powerful one because it allowed humanity to advance in some way: to
communicate more accurately, to understand the natural world, to master the
natural world. Michael Young, who in the 1970s argued for the socially
constructed nature of all knowledge, argues now that:

> although we cannot deny the sociality of all forms of knowledge, certain
> forms of knowledge which I find useful to refer to as powerful knowledge
> and are often equated with 'knowledge itself', have properties that are
> emergent from and not wholly dependent on their social and historical
> origins.[42]

Giving all pupils the chance to understand this powerful knowledge and
practise using it has democratic and egalitarian benefits, as well as long-run
economic benefits.

What about the claim that this type of curriculum is a curriculum of the
elite? That, as Martin Johnson has argued, it forces working-class pupils to
learn inappropriate and irrelevant upper-class knowledge? The idea that there
is such a thing as upper-class knowledge is demonstrably false. As Jonathan
Rose rather pithily puts it, 'if the dominant class defines high culture, then how
do we explain the passionate pursuit of knowledge by proletarian autodidacts,
not to mention the pervasive philistinism of the British aristocracy?'[43] Indeed,
both the Queen Mother and Michael Faraday are just two historical figures
who offer fairly convincing empirical rebuttal of Johnson's sweeping statement.
Among my own friends are many people from fairly modest backgrounds who
I feel confident have a better understanding of high culture than Prince Harry,
for example.

When you examine it at all, the idea that high culture *belongs* to any class or
culture is of course ridiculous. Civilisation has progressed through the
inventions and breakthroughs of many individuals and many collections of
individuals. Some of the most important and groundbreaking inventions were
made by people whose names and histories we will never know. These

breakthroughs are a part of the common inheritance of humanity, and do not belong to a particular culture or nation. Are we not going to teach indigenous British pupils how to count because the Hindu and Arabic origins of the numbering system mean it is irrelevant to their culture? Are we to argue that drama composed in Attic caves thousands of years ago is somehow *owned* by a modern-day British upper class? One of Johnson's fellow trade unionists, Robert Tressell, shows why such arguments are false:

> What we call civilisation—the accumulation of knowledge which has come down to us from our forefathers—is the fruit of thousands of years of human thought and toil. It is not the result of the labour of the ancestors of any separate class of people who exist today, and therefore it is by right the common heritage of all. Every little child that is born into the world, no matter whether he is clever or dull, whether he is physically perfect or lame, or blind; no matter how much he may excel or fall short of his fellows in other respects, in one thing at least he is their equal—he is one of the heirs of all the ages that have gone before.[44]

In his book, *The Intellectual Life of the British Working Classes*, Jonathan Rose documents the extraordinary extent of working-class autodidacticism in the late nineteenth and early twentieth century.[45] The mill-workers, coal-miners and flower-sellers who spent their spare time producing Shakespeare plays and reading classic works of literature did not think that literature was part of someone else's culture. On the contrary, as I argued earlier, they believed in an idea of relevance far more broad-minded than the narrow and crippling one we have in schools today. Shakespeare, Dickens and Milton *were* relevant to them. Will Crooks, another member of the early Labour movement (and the fourth Labour MP) recalled reading the *Iliad* for the first time:

> On my way home from work one Saturday afternoon I was lucky enough to pick up Homer's 'Iliad' for twopence at an old bookstall. After dinner I took it upstairs — we were able to afford an upstairs room by that time — and read it lying on the bed. What a revelation it was to me! Pictures of romance and beauty I had never dreamed of suddenly opened up before my eyes. I was transported from the East End to an enchanted land. It was a rare luxury to a working lad like me just home from work to find myself suddenly among the heroes and nymphs and gods of ancient Greece.[46]

For Martin Johnson, however, knowledge such as the *Iliad* does not belong to people from Crooks's social class, and should not be taught to them. For Johnson, the determinant for whether you receive an education full of powerful knowledge or not is the social class of your parents. As he argued, high culture 'in reality is closely related to the lifestyle of an upper class'.[47] His entire criticism of twentieth-century mass education is that it 'copied the curriculum considered necessary for social elites: leisured classes who could afford and valued such attitudes'.[48] For me, that was the triumph of twentieth-century mass education. Whereas previously only the leisured classes had the time for a good general education, in the twentieth century, thanks to the hard work of people like Crooks and Tressell, everyone had a primary and then a secondary education provided for them for free.

It is sometimes said that those who want to teach knowledge want to take us back to the nineteenth century. In fact the reverse is true. It is those who do not want to teach knowledge who want to take us back to the nineteenth century. For when we consider the nineteenth century, we see that many of the elites and bureaucrats at the time were extremely reluctant to teach knowledge to the masses, on the grounds that it would make them 'refractory' and 'seditious'. Here is an argument by Davies Giddy from Hansard in 1807:

> Giving education to the labouring classes of the poor ... would, in effect, be found to be prejudicial to their morals and happiness; it would teach them to despise their lot in life, instead of making them good servants in agriculture, and other laborious employments to which their rank in society had destined them; instead of teaching them subordination, it would render them factious and refractory, as was evident in the manufacturing counties it would enable them to read seditious pamphlets, vicious books, and publications against Christianity.[49]

If we look back at the late nineteenth and early twentieth century, we find that those who wanted to restrict mass education were the ultra-conservative, who feared that extending powerful knowledge to the masses would challenge the unequal basis of society. Both conservatives and progressives could agree that knowledge was empowering. Knowledge was the way to change things. That is why progressives were in favour of extending knowledge to the masses and conservatives were not, and that is why one of the key goals of the early Labour movement was free education. There is nothing elitist about powerful knowledge. What is elitist is the suggestion that such knowledge belongs to an elite. It is baffling to think about why people in the modern British Labour movement have assumed the same ideas as ultra-conservatives from nearly two centuries ago.

Rather than consider the reasons for that, I want now to look to the United States, where elements of the progressive movement are still animated by the spirit that inspired Crooks and Tressell. For the American educationalist E.D. Hirsch, ensuring that all pupils have access to knowledge is a question of social justice, and, as he notes, 'the traditional forms of literate culture are precisely the most effective instruments for political and social change'.[50] In a fascinating passage, he proves this by quoting from some 1970s issues of *The Black Panther*, the newspaper of the most radical section of the civil rights movement. He notes that all their radical and revolutionary writing depends a great deal on this shared body of knowledge, and that their methods of expressing themselves are undoubtedly conservative. Hirsch states that he has not found 'a single misspelled word in the many pages of radical sentiment' he has examined.[51] His conclusion is that 'to be a conservative in the means of communication is the road to effectiveness in modern life, in whatever direction one wishes to be effective'.[52]

Hirsch put these theories into practice by designing a curriculum that would aim to teach pupils this important knowledge. Known as the Core Knowledge curriculum, it contains detailed and carefully sequenced guidelines explaining what pupils need to learn in each year from kindergarten to grade 8 (the equivalent of years 1–9 in English terms). I first encountered Hirsch's curriculum after three years of teaching the English curriculum. It is fair to say it was an on-first-looking-into-Chapman's-Homer moment. I was incredibly impressed by the range of content. In language arts (the American equivalent of English literature and language), the curriculum included short stories by, among others, Chekhov, Hawthorne and Tolstoy; poetry by Emily Dickinson, Carl Sandburg and Robert Browning; lists of words that pupils should be able to spell; grammatical terms they should be able to understand and use; and commonly used foreign phrases they should be able to understand. The history curriculum is designed to be coherent and cumulative – that is, instead of studying randomly selected periods of history from term to term, pupils start in first grade studying the first American peoples, and then progress up to the present day, which they reach in the eighth grade. World history runs alongside this, beginning with the Ancient Greeks and progressing to industrialism, the French Revolution and Latin American independence movements. In grade 7, American and world history are combined so that the last 100 years are taught from a global perspective. These two grades include topics on World War II in Europe and at Home, 1939–45 and the Decline of European Colonialism. I realised with a shock that American 14-year-old pupils studying this curriculum would end up with a better understanding of British history than most English 16-year-olds.[53]

In the United States, individual schools in most states are free to adopt their own curriculum. In the variety of different schools where Hirsch's curriculum has been used, it has proved incredibly successful.[54] Most strikingly, it was used as the basis for Massachusetts's highly successful curriculum reforms of the early 1990s, which are described here by Sol Stern:

> The 'Massachusetts miracle', in which Bay State students' soaring test scores broke records, was the direct consequence of the state legislature's passage of the 1993 Education Reform Act, which established knowledge-based standards for all grades and a rigorous testing system linked to the new standards. And those standards, Massachusetts reformers have acknowledged, are Hirsch's legacy.
>
> Hirsch's theories, long merely persuasive, now have solid empirical backing in Massachusetts's miraculous educational reforms. Before the

state passed its reform legislation, school districts employed a hodgepodge of instructional approaches, had no standard curriculum, and neglected academic content. But one element of the 1993 Education Reform Act was Hirschean knowledge-based curricula for each grade …

In the new millennium, Massachusetts students have surged upward on the biennial National Assessment of Educational Progress (NAEP)—'the nation's report card,' as education scholars call it. On the 2005 NAEP tests, Massachusetts ranked first in the nation in fourth- and eighth-grade reading and fourth- and eighth-grade math. It then repeated the feat in 2007. No state had ever scored first in both grades and both subjects in a single year—let alone for two consecutive test cycles. On another reliable test, the Trends in International Math and Science Studies, the state's fourth-graders last year ranked second globally in science and third in math, while the eighth-graders tied for first in science and placed sixth in math. (States can volunteer, as Massachusetts did, to have their students compared with national averages.) The United States as a whole finished tenth.[55]

In 2008, the Core Knowledge Foundation designed a reading programme that featured texts and teaching resources based on the Core Knowledge curriculum.[56] This programme was piloted in New York for three years with pupils from kindergarten to second grade and compared with balanced literacy reading programmes, which promote generic reading strategies. The results were published in March 2012:

> The study found that second graders who were taught to read using the Core Knowledge program scored significantly higher on reading comprehension tests than did those in the comparison schools.[57]

The principal of one of the schools involved praised the effect it had on poorer students:

> 'For my children, who are economically disadvantaged, they needed something more, and the Core Knowledge pilot had it,' Ms. Grady said. Of the nearly 700 students enrolled at her school last year, 88 percent met the city's definition of poverty.[58]

One of the most difficult tasks for any education reform is closing the achievement gap between higher and lower achievers. Even very effective programmes can struggle to do this. With the Core Knowledge reading programme, not only did all the pupils improve their reading scores across the three years of the pilot, but the effects were strongest for pupils with lower incoming scores.[59]

Partly as a result of this success, large sections of the American left have enthusiastically welcomed Hirsch's curriculum. Most strikingly, the American

Federation of Teachers (AFT), America's second-largest teaching union, are four-square behind his ideas and his curriculum. The AFT are no right-wing front organisation. In fact, they have partnered with our own National Union of Teachers (NUT) to share tactics on how to fight against free schools and charters. In June 2012, the Deputy General Secretary of the NUT, Kevin Courtney, praised the valuable insight he had gained from talking to AFT members in Baltimore and Philadelphia.[60]

As well as opposing charter schools, the AFT have also spent a great deal of time and energy supporting Hirsch's Core Knowledge curriculum. The President of the AFT, Randi Weingarten, has frequently spoken of the benefits of the Core Knowledge curriculum. She wrote this blurb for Hirsch's latest book: 'now more than ever we need his lessons to become part of our common wisdom'.[61] The Secretary-Treasurer of the AFT, Toni Cortese, is a trustee of the Common Core Foundation, an organisation that supports knowledge-rich curricula.[62] The AFT journal, *American Educator*, often publishes articles by Hirsch and other leading lights of the Core Knowledge Foundation.[63] Diane Ravitch, who is perhaps the foremost critic of charter and free schools anywhere in the world, is a long-standing and vocal supporter of Core Knowledge. Indeed, she was the person who persuaded Hirsch to write *Cultural Literacy*.[64] Hirsch himself is a Democrat, has described himself as a quasi-socialist and dedicated one of his books to Antonio Gramsci, who has been a significant influence on his thought.[65]

In short, there are strong progressive reasons to support the teaching of knowledge, and progressives both past and present have recognised this. Knowledge doesn't indoctrinate; knowledge liberates.

Notes

1   Berger, P.L. and Luckmann, T. *The Social Construction of Reality: A Treatise in the Sociology of Knowledge*. London: Penguin Books, 1991.
2   Young, M. (ed.). *Knowledge and Control: New Directions for the Sociology of Education*. London: Collier Macmillan, 1971.
3   Young, M. An approach to the study of curricula as socially organised knowledge. In: Young, M. (ed.) *Knowledge and Control: New Directions for the Sociology of Education*. London: Collier Macmillan, 1971, p. 32.
4   Apple, M. *Ideology and Curriculum*. 3rd edn. New York: RoutledgeFalmer, 2004, p. 4.
5   Kelly, A.V. *The Curriculum: Theory and Practice*. 6th edn. London: SAGE, 2009, p. 40.
6   Ibid., p. 41.
7   Whitty, G. *Sociology and School Knowledge: Curriculum Theory, Research, and Politics* London: Methuen, 1985, p. 2.
8   White, J. What schools are for and why. Impact No. 14 (2007), pp. 2 and 22, www.philosophy-of-education.org/uploads/14_white.pdf (accessed 6 March 2013).

9   Association of Teachers and Lecturers. Subject to change: new thinking on the curriculum (2007), pp. 72 and 101, www.atl.org.uk/Images/Subject%20to%20 change.pdf (accessed 6 March 2013).

10 Ibid., p. 61

11 *Telegraph*. Schools should teach skills, not subjects (2008), www.telegraph.co.uk/ news/uknews/2071224/Schools-should-teach-skills-not-subjects.html (accessed 6 March 2013); White, J. What schools are for and why. Impact No. 14 (2007), pp. 2, 20–23, www.philosophy-of-education.org/uploads/14_white.pdf (accessed 6 March 2013).

12 Apple, M. *Ideology and Curriculum*. 3rd edn. New York: RoutledgeFalmer, 2004.

13 From information about the sixth edition: 'A very well-respected book [and a] Curriculum classic … [which offers] balance to current official publications … One of its strengths is the coherent argument that runs throughout. It is very much a product of the wide knowledge and experience of the author.' Jenny Houssart, Senior Lecturer, Department of Learning, Curriculum & Communication, Institute of Education, University of London, UK.

14 *Telegraph*. Schools should teach skills, not subjects (2008), www.telegraph.co.uk/ news/uknews/2071224/Schools-should-teach-skills-not-subjects.html (accessed 6 March 2013)

15 Kelly, A.V. *The Curriculum: Theory and Practice*. 6th edn. London: SAGE, 2009, p. 40.

16 White, J. What schools are for and why. Impact No. 14 (2007), p. 47, www. philosophy-of-education.org/uploads/14_white.pdf (accessed 6 March 2013).

17 Brown, M. and White, J. An unstable framework – Critical perspectives on the framework for the National Curriculum (2012), www.newvisionsforeducation. org.uk/2012/04/05/an-unstable-framework/ (accessed 6 March 2012).

18 Office for Standards in Education, Children's Services and Skills. Moving English forward: Action to raise standards in English (2012), p. 23, www.ofsted.gov.uk/ resources/moving-english-forward (accessed 6 March 2013).

19 Office for Standards in Education. Children's Services and Skills. Making a mark: art, craft and design education 2008–11 (2012), p. 38, www.ofsted.gov.uk/ resources/making-mark-art-craft-and-design-education-2008-11   (accessed   6 March 2013).

20 Office for Standards in Education, Children's Services and Skills. Transforming religious education: Religious education in schools 2006   09 (2010), p. 15, www. ofsted.gov.uk/resources/transforming-religious-education (accessed on 6 March 2013).

21 Office for Standards in Education, Children's Services and Skills. Excellence in English: What we can learn from 12 outstanding schools (2011), p. 16, www. ofsted.gov.uk/resources/excellence-english (accessed 6 March 2013).

22 Office for Standards in Education, Children's Services and Skills. Moving English forward: Action to raise standards in English (2012), p. 23, www.ofsted.gov.uk/ resources/moving-english-forward (accessed 6 March 2013).

23 Office for Standards in Education, Children's Services and Skills. Moving English forward: Action to raise standards in English (2012), pp. 4, 23, 32, 52, www.ofsted. gov.uk/resources/moving-english-forward (accessed 6 March 2013).

24 See the book's Appendix, available at: http://www.routledge.com/books/ details/9780415746823. The lessons or units numbered 2–6, 8, 9, 11, 14, 19, 22, 25, 26 and 32 involve some mention of literary or grammatical content.

25 White, J. What schools are for and why. Impact No. 14 (2007), p. 12, www. philosophy-of-education.org/uploads/14_white.pdf (accessed 6 March 2013).

26 Brown, M. and White, J. An unstable framework – Critical perspectives on the framework for the National Curriculum (2012), www.newvisionsforeducation. org.uk/2012/04/05/an-unstable-framework/ (accessed 6 March 2012).

27 Tawney, R.H. *The Radical Tradition: Twelve Essays on Politics, Education and Literature*. Harmondsworth: Penguin, 1966, pp. 87–88.

28 Beveridge, W. *Full Employment in a Free Society: A Report*. London: George Allen and Unwin, 1944, p. 380.

29 Jefferson, T. Letter to Charles Yancey (6 January 1816) (2012), www.monticello. org/site/jefferson/quotations-education (accessed 6 March 2013).

30 Hansard Society. Audit of Political Engagement 10: The 2013 Report (2013), p. 35, http://tinyurl.com/lvc6mlf (accessed 20 May 2013).

31 Ibid., p. 33.

32 Willingham, D.T. *Why Don't Students Like School?* San Francisco: Jossey-Bass, 2009, p. 47.

33 Ibid.

34 Willinsky, J. The vocabulary of cultural literacy in a newspaper of substance. Paper presented at the Annual Meeting of the National Reading Conference, 29 November–3 December 1988, Tucson, Arizona, USA; Hirsch, E.D., Kett, J.F and Trefil, J.S. *The New Dictionary of Cultural Literacy*. Boston: Houghton Mifflin, 2002.

35 Core Knowledge Foundation. Core Knowledge at a Glance (2013), http://www. coreknowledge.org/media (accessed 6 March 2013); Stern, S.E.D. Hirsch's curriculum for democracy (2009), www.city-journal.org/2009/19_4_hirsch.html (accessed 6 March 2013).

36 Transcription of an address delivered by Maya Angelou at the 1985 National Assembly of Local Arts Agencies, Cedar Rapids, Iowa, USA, 12 June 1985; Garber, M. *Profiling Shakespeare*. New York: Routledge, 2008, p. 117.

37 *Guardian*. British Museum Shakespeare exhibition to include prized Robben Island copy (2012), www.guardian.co.uk/culture/2012/jul/17/british-museum-shake speare-exhibition-robben-island (accessed 6 March 2013).

38 BBC Radio Four. Shakespeare's Restless World: Shakespeare Goes Global (2012), www.bbc.co.uk/radio4/features/shakespeares-restless-world/transcripts/ shakespearegoesglobal/ (accessed 6 March 2013).

39 Willingham, D.T. *Why Don't Students Like School?* San Francisco: Jossey-Bass, 2009, p. 48.

40 Ibid.

41 Common Core Foundation. Why we're behind: What top nations teach their students but we don't (2009), www.commoncore.org/_docs/CCreport_ whybehind.pdf (accessed 4 March 2013); Ruddock, G. and Sainsbury, M. Comparison of the core primary curriculum in England to those of other high performing countries (2008), www.education.gov.uk/publications/eOrdering Download/DCSF-RW048v2.pdf (accessed 6 March 2013).

42 Young, M. Curriculum theory and the problem of knowledge: a personal journey and an unfinished project. In: Short, E.C. and Waks, L.J. *Leaders in Curriculum Studies: Intellectual Self-Portraits*. Rotterdam: Sense Publishers, 2009, p. 220.

43 Rose, J. *The Intellectual Life of the British Working Classes*. New Haven: Yale University Press, 2002, p. 4.

44 Tressell, R. *The Ragged Trousered Philanthropists*. Oxford: Oxford University Press, 2005, p. 23.

45 Rose, J. *The Intellectual Life of the British Working Classes*. New Haven: Yale University Press, 2002, p. 4.

46 Haw, G. *From Workhouse to Westminster: The Life Story of Will Crooks, M.P.* London: Cassell, 1907, p. 23.

47 Association of Teachers and Lecturers. Subject to change: new thinking on the curriculum (2007), p. 101, www.atl.org.uk/Images/Subject%20to%20change.pdf (accessed 6 March 2013).

48 Ibid.

49 Davies, G. Parochial Schools Bill. Hansard, 9: cc798–806, 13 June 1807 (2013), http://hansard.millbanksystems.com/commons/1807/aug/04/parochial-schools-bill (accessed 6 March 2013).

50 Hirsch, E.D. *Cultural Literacy: What Every American Needs to Know*. Boston: Houghton Mifflin, 1987, p. 22.

51 Ibid., p. 23.

52 Ibid.

53 Core Knowledge Foundation. Core Knowledge Sequence: Content and Skill Guidelines for Grades K–8, Core Knowledge Foundation, 2010 (2010), www.coreknowledge.org/mimik/mimik_uploads/documents/480/CKFSequence_Rev.pdf (accessed 6 March 2013).

54 Core Knowledge Foundation. How Do We Know This Works? An Overview of Research on Core Knowledge (2004), www.coreknowledge.org/mimik/mimik_uploads/documents/106/How%20Do%20We%20Know%20This%20Works.pdf (accessed 6 March 2013).

55 Stern, S.E.D. Hirsch's curriculum for democracy (2009), www.city-journal.org/2009/19_4_hirsch.html (accessed 6 March 2013).

56 Education News. An Interview with Matthew Davis: Core Knowledge in New York City (2008), www.educationnews.org/articles/28832/1/An-Interview-with-Matthew-Davis-Core-Knowledge-in-New-York-City/Page1.html (accessed 6 March 2013).

57 *The New York Times*. Nonfiction curriculum enhanced reading skills, study finds (2012), www.nytimes.com/2012/03/12/nyregion/nonfiction-curriculum-enhanced-reading-skills-in-new-york-city-schools.html?_r=3&ref=education&%20Accessed& (accessed 6 March 2013).

58 Ibid.

59 Research and Policy Support Group. *Evaluating the NYC Core Knowledge Early Literacy Pilot: Year 3 Report*. New York: New York Department of Education, p. 10.

60 American Federation of Teachers. International Update: The AFT at work in the world (2012), www.aft.org/pdfs/international/AFT_NUT_report0912.pdf (accessed 6 March 2013).

61 Hirsch, E.D. *The Making of Americans: Democracy and our Schools.* New Haven: Yale University Press, 2009, back cover.

62 Common Core. Profile of Antonia Cortese (2011), www.commoncore.org/wwa-trust-ac.php (accessed 6 March 2013).

63 American Federation of Teachers. *American Educator.* Index of Authors, (F–J) (2013), www.aft.org/newspubs/periodicals/ae/authors2.cfm (accessed 6 March 2013).

64 The Core Knowledge Blog. The Sharpton–Klein education reform agenda. Guest blogger: Diane Ravitch (2008), http://blog.coreknowledge.org/2008/06/23/the-sharpton-klein-education-reform-agenda/ (accessed 6 March 2013).

65 Education Sector. Core convictions: An interview with E.D. Hirsch (2006), www.educationsector.org/publications/core-convictions (accessed 6 March 2013); Hirsch, E.D., *The Schools We Need and Why We Don't Have Them.* New York: Anchor, 1999, pp. 6–7.

Conclusion

Throughout this book, I have tried to stress that I share the aims of many of the people whose methods I disagree with. I agree that education should aim to produce confident, creative and problem-solving critical thinkers. I agree that we should prepare pupils for the twenty-first century. I agree that we should design our education system to suit everyone, not just the high achievers. I agree that education should be concerned with democracy and equality. I agree that pupils should be active learners and that lessons should be engaging. It is because I believe all of these things that I am so concerned about the current education system. The methods we are currently using to achieve these aims simply do not work.

The main reason they do not work is because of a misguided, outdated and pseudo-scientific stigma against the teaching of knowledge. The evidence for the importance of knowledge is clear. We have a strong theoretical model that explains why knowledge is at the heart of cognition. We have strong empirical evidence about the success of curricula that teach knowledge. And we have strong empirical evidence about the success of pedagogy that promotes the effective transmission of knowledge. If we fail to teach knowledge, pupils fail to learn.

But, as we have also seen, very little of this evidence is known or taught within the English education system. The implications of this are astonishing. It is not simply a matter of saying that we have got a few bits of obscure theory wrong. People were rightly shocked when Ben Goldacre exposed the way that the pseudo-scientific Brain Gym programme had worked its way into so many schools.[1] But what we are looking at here is something far worse. The fundamental ideas of our education system are flawed. When one looks at the scientific evidence about how the brain learns and at the design of our education system, one is forced to conclude that the system actively retards education. If our curriculum were to promote learning, then it would specify a core, coherent and sequenced body of knowledge. Instead, it specifies no knowledge and suggests that the knowledge that is taught is unimportant in comparison to skills. If our pedagogy were to promote learning, then it would recognise the importance of teacher-led instruction and guided practice. Instead, teachers are advised not to direct their pupils and are encouraged to facilitate unguided projects. If our schools wanted to ensure that all pupils could read effectively by the time they were 16, then they would focus on gradually building up the amount of important cultural knowledge pupils knew. Instead, schools teach random and often trivial bits of information, many of which the pupils know already.

I want to speak more anecdotally now about my personal experience of working in a system that promoted such false theories. In Chapter 7, I discussed the way that many educational theorists used the concept of hegemony to explain the way that certain ideas and practices become accepted by people within an institution. Hegemony is a useful concept. I would argue that the myths I have discussed here are hegemonic within the education system. It is hard to have a discussion about education without sooner or later hitting one of these myths. As theorists of hegemony realise, the most powerful thing about hegemonic ideas is that they seem to be natural common sense. They are just a normal part of everyday life. This makes them exceptionally difficult to challenge, because it does not seem as if there is anything there to challenge.

However, as the theorists of hegemony also realised, hegemonic ideas depend on certain unseen processes. One tactic is the suppression of all evidence that contradicts them. I trained as a teacher, taught for three years, attended numerous in-service training days, wrote several essays about education and followed educational policy closely without ever even encountering any of the evidence about knowledge I speak of here, let alone actually hearing anyone advocate it. John Hattie's description of the anger his trainees felt at hearing about the success of direct instruction applied to me too. For three years I struggled to improve my pupils' education without ever knowing that I could be using hugely more effective methods. I would spend entire lessons quietly observing my pupils chatting away in groups about complete misconceptions and I would think that the problem in the lesson was that I had been too prescriptive. We need to reform the main teacher training and inspection agencies so that they stop promoting completely discredited ideas and give more space to theories with much greater scientific backing.

However, at its heart this is a problem of ideas, not institutions. In the introduction, I spoke of Keynes's analysis of the influence of ideas. Whilst some institutional and structural reform may be valuable, what needs to change most of all is our reliance on defunct ideas. At stake is the education of all our pupils, and particularly the education of our least advantaged pupils. Unless we place the powerful and liberating force of knowledge at the heart of our education system, it will continue to fail our pupils and to deepen inequality.

Note

1   Goldacre, B. *Bad Science*. London: Fourth Estate, 2008, pp. 13–20.

Index